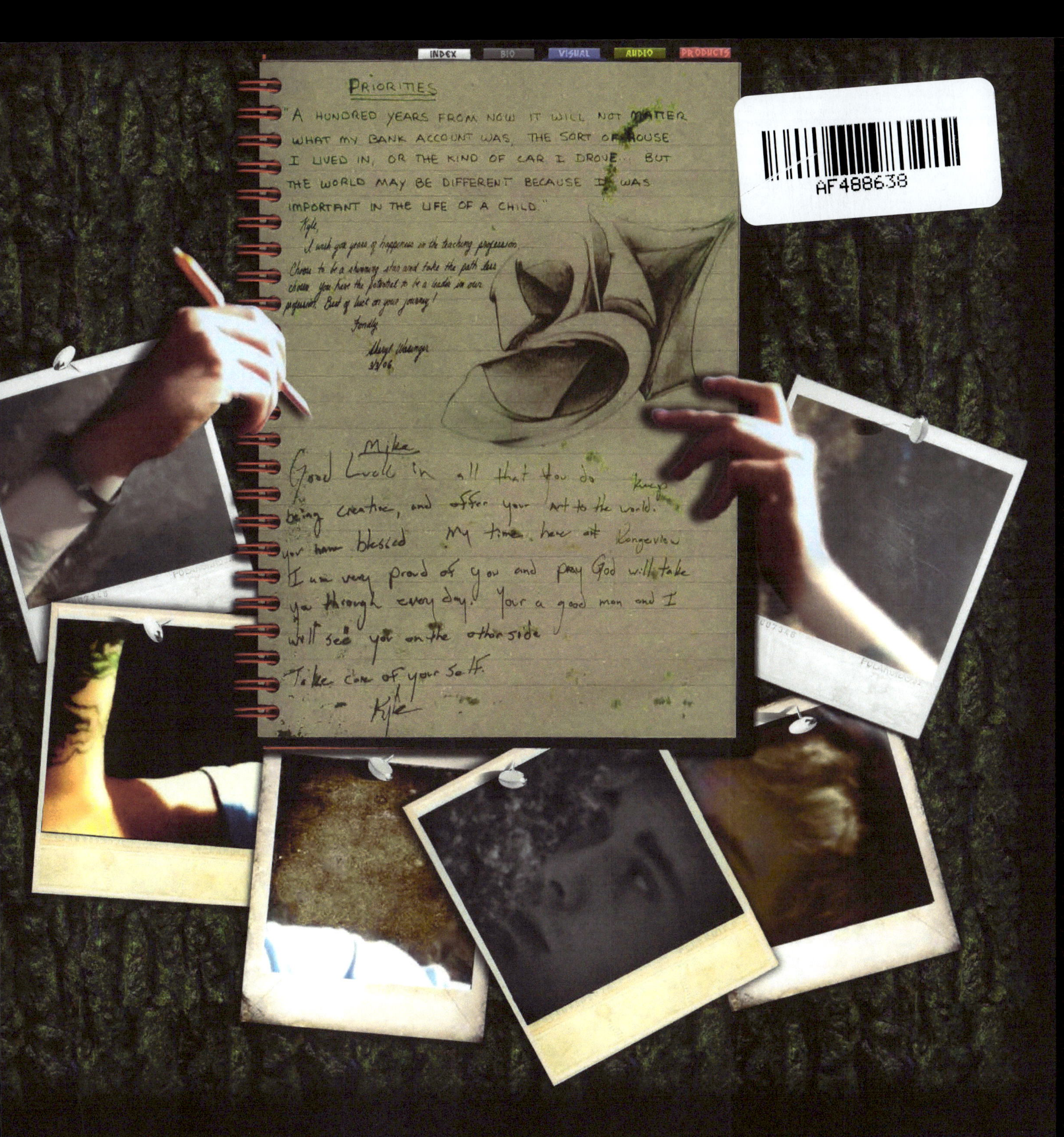

INDEX   BIO   VISUAL   AUDIO   PRODUCTS

PRIORITIES

"A HUNDRED YEARS FROM NOW IT WILL NOT MATTER
WHAT MY BANK ACCOUNT WAS, THE SORT OF HOUSE
I LIVED IN, OR THE KIND OF CAR I DROVE... BUT
THE WORLD MAY BE DIFFERENT BECAUSE I WAS
IMPORTANT IN THE LIFE OF A CHILD."

Kyle,
I wish you years of happiness in the teaching profession.
Choose to be a shining star and take the path less
chosen. You have the potential to be a leader in our
profession. Best of luck on your journey!
Fondly,

AF488638

Mike
Good Luck in all that you do keep
being creative, and offer your Art to the world.
You have blessed My times here at Longeview
I am very proud of you and pray God will take
you through every day. Your a good man and I
will see you on the other side

Take care of your self.
Kyle

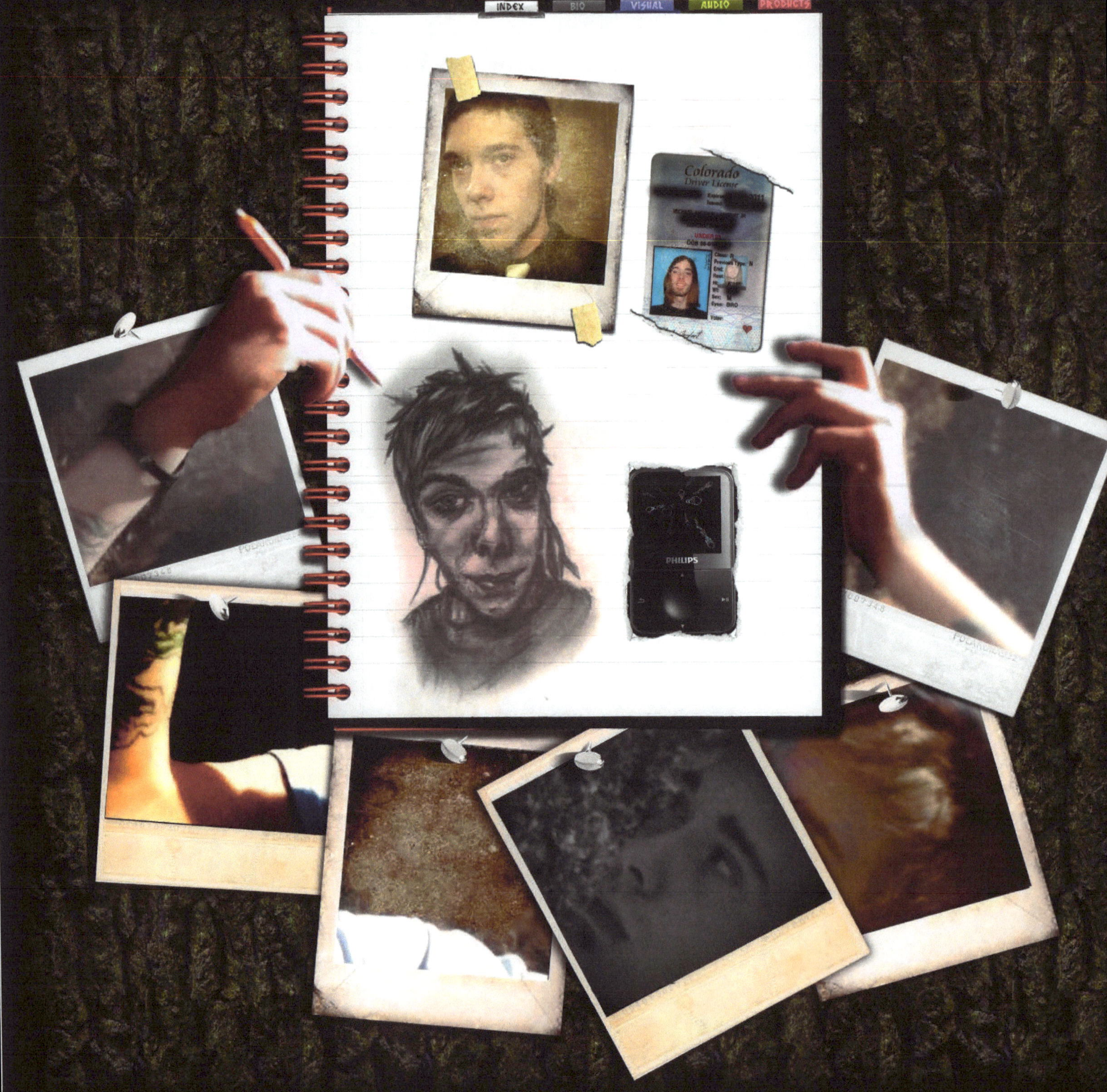

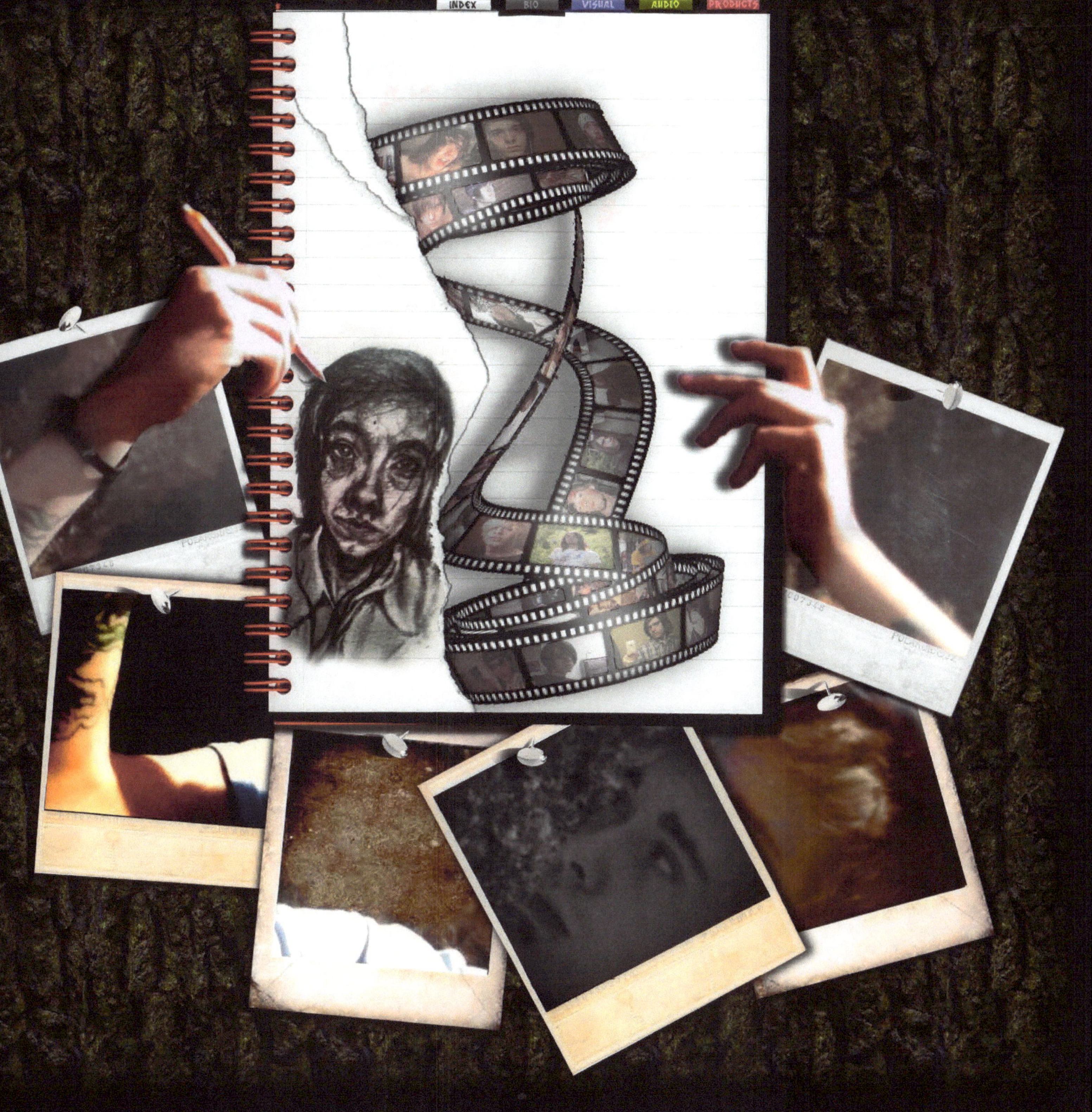

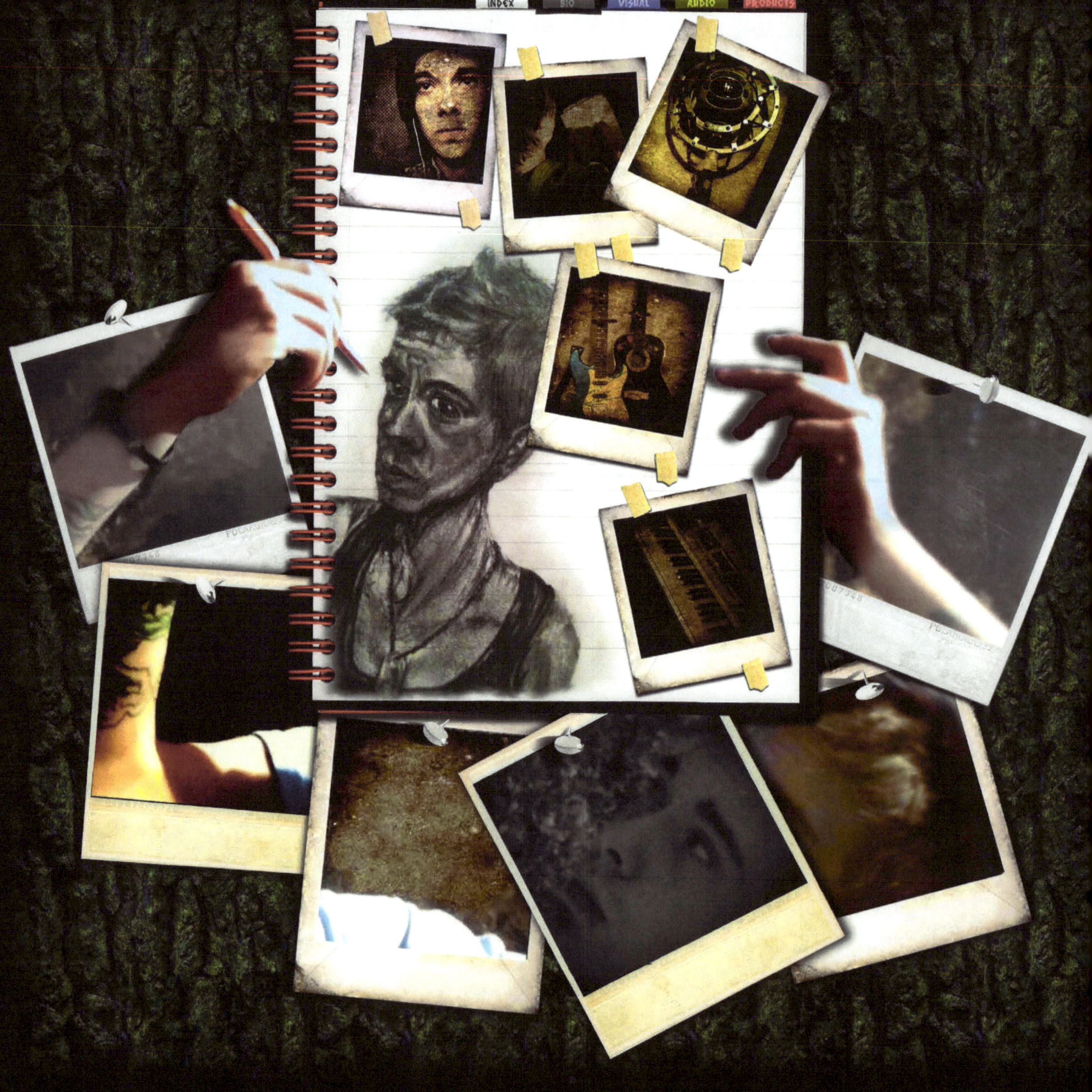

INDEX
BIO
VISUAL
AUDIO
PRODUCTS

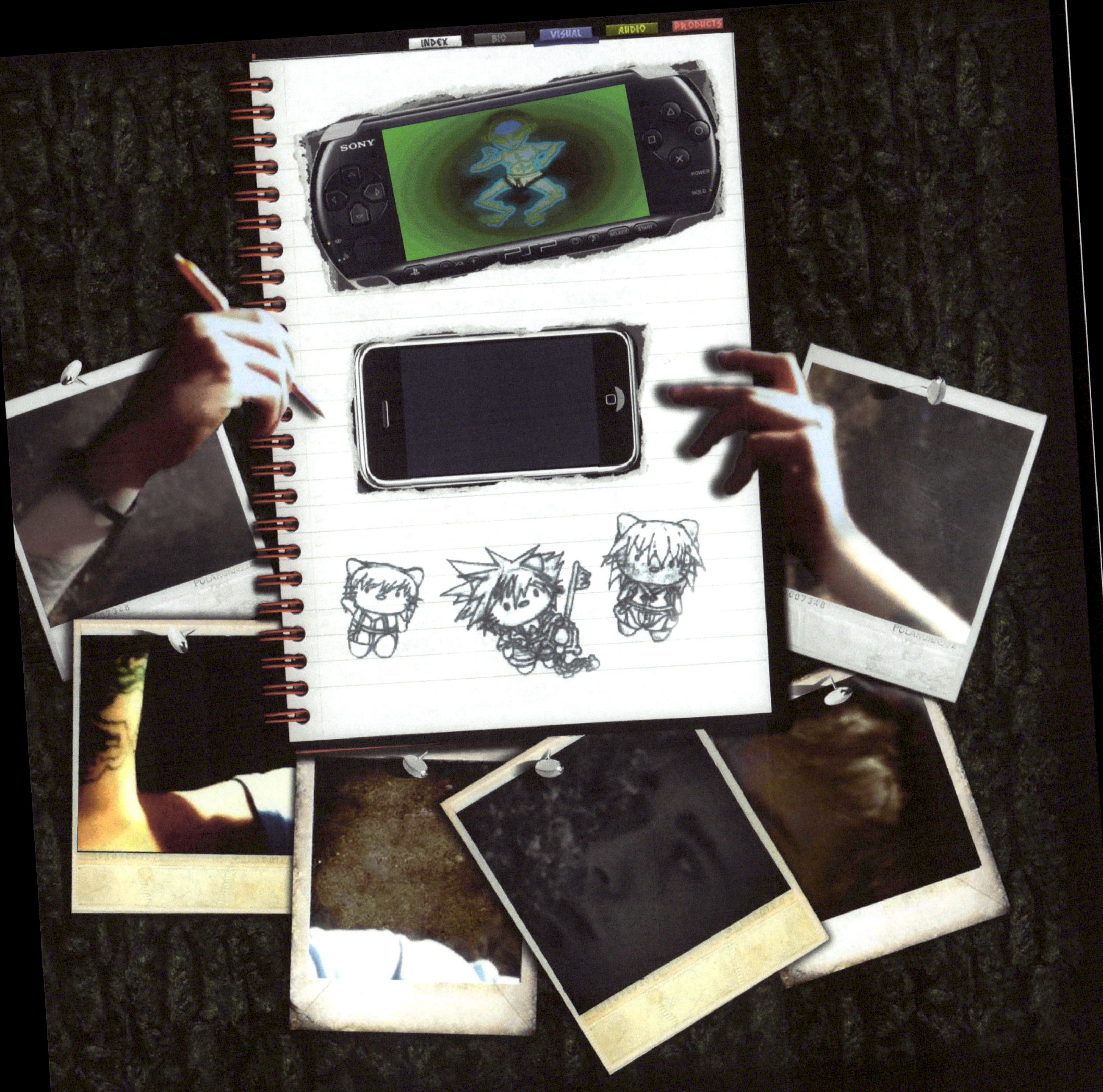

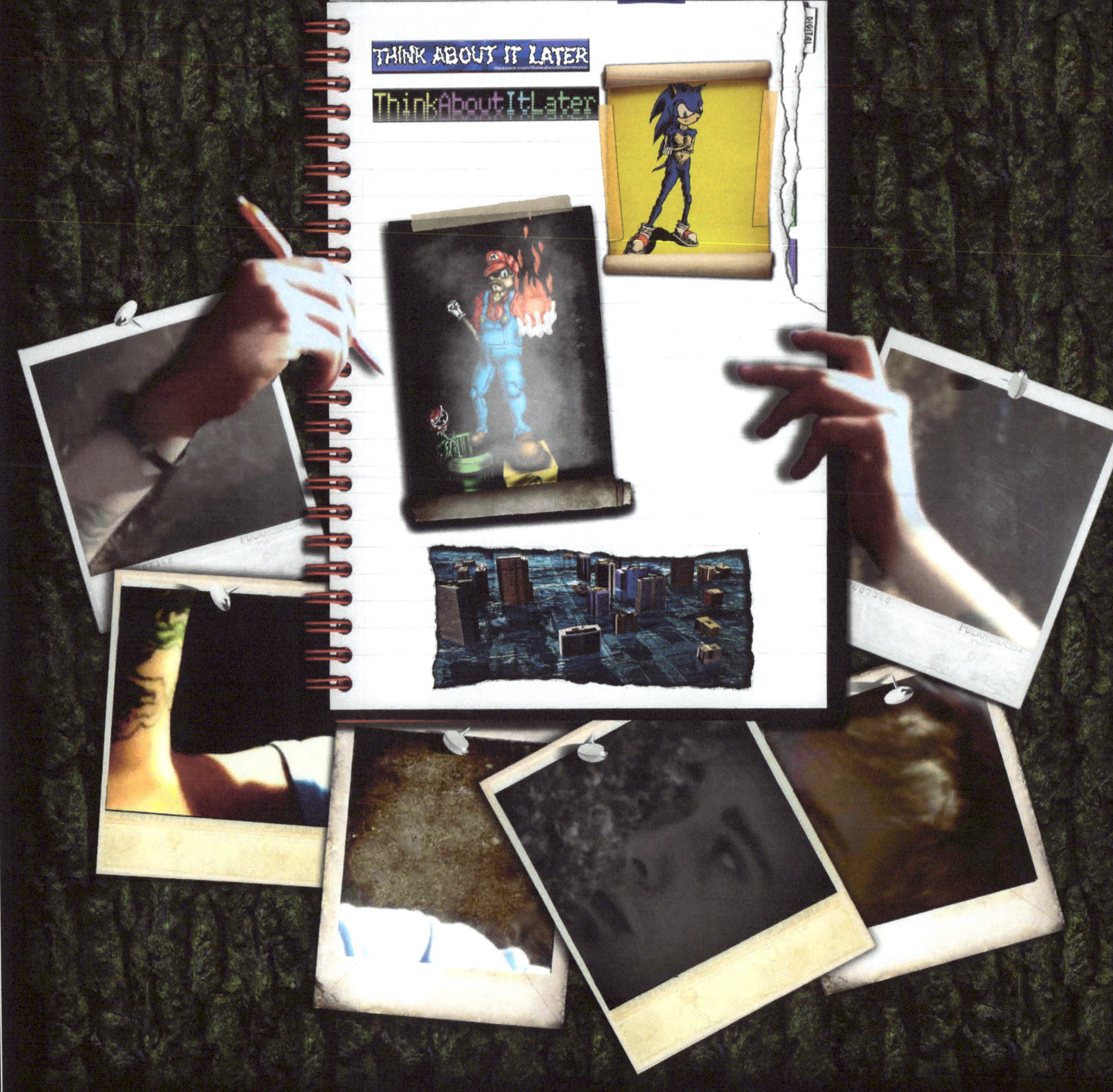
INDEX
BIO
VISUAL
AUDIO
PRODUCTS
DIGITAL
THINK ABOUT IT LATER
myspace.com/thinkaboutitlatermusic
ThinkAboutItLater

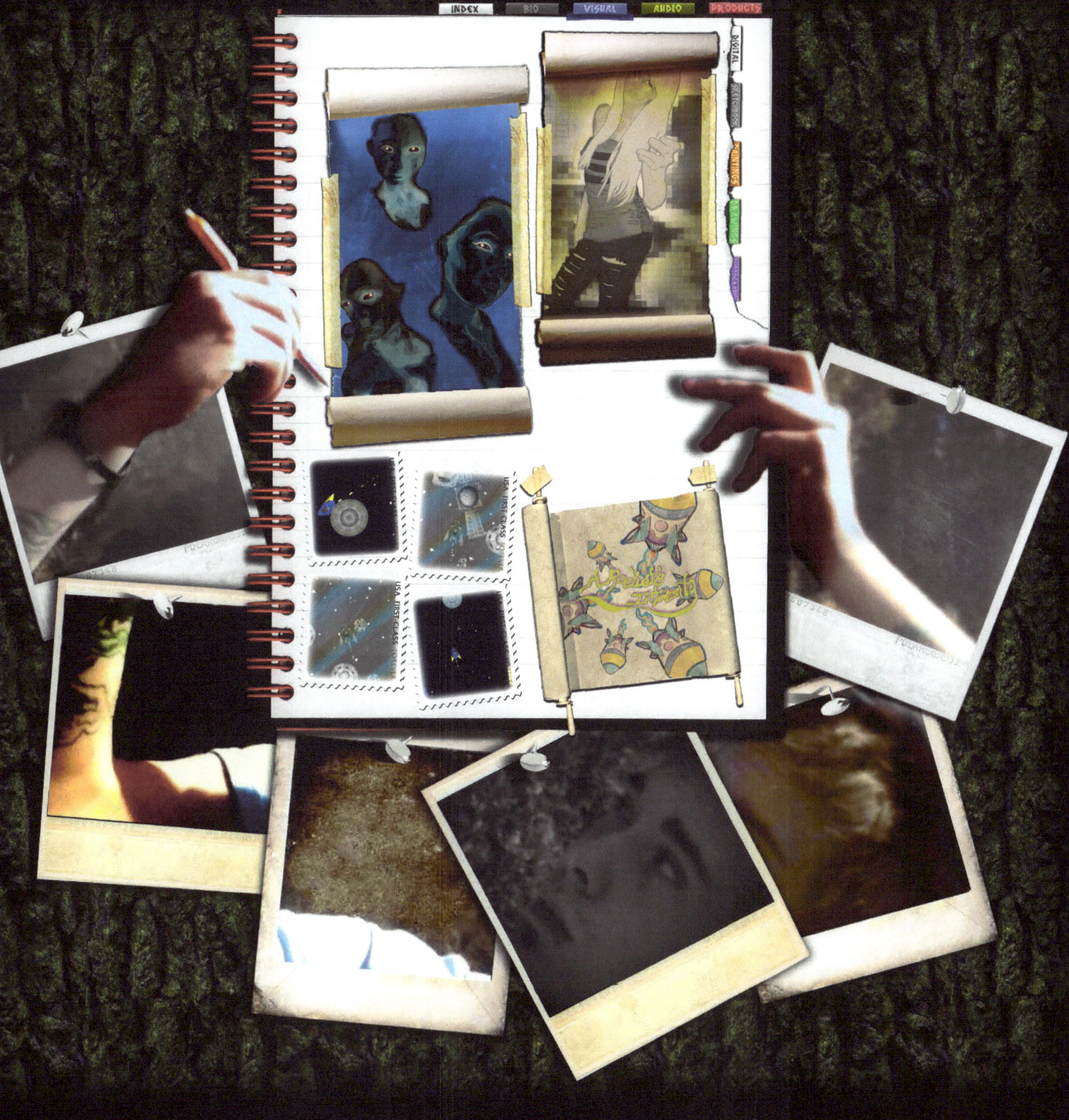

INDEX
BIO
VISUAL
AUDIO
PRODUCTS
DIGITAL
SKETCHBOOK
PAINTINGS
DRAWINGS
PHOTOGRAPHY
USA FIRST-CLASS
USA FIRST-CLASS

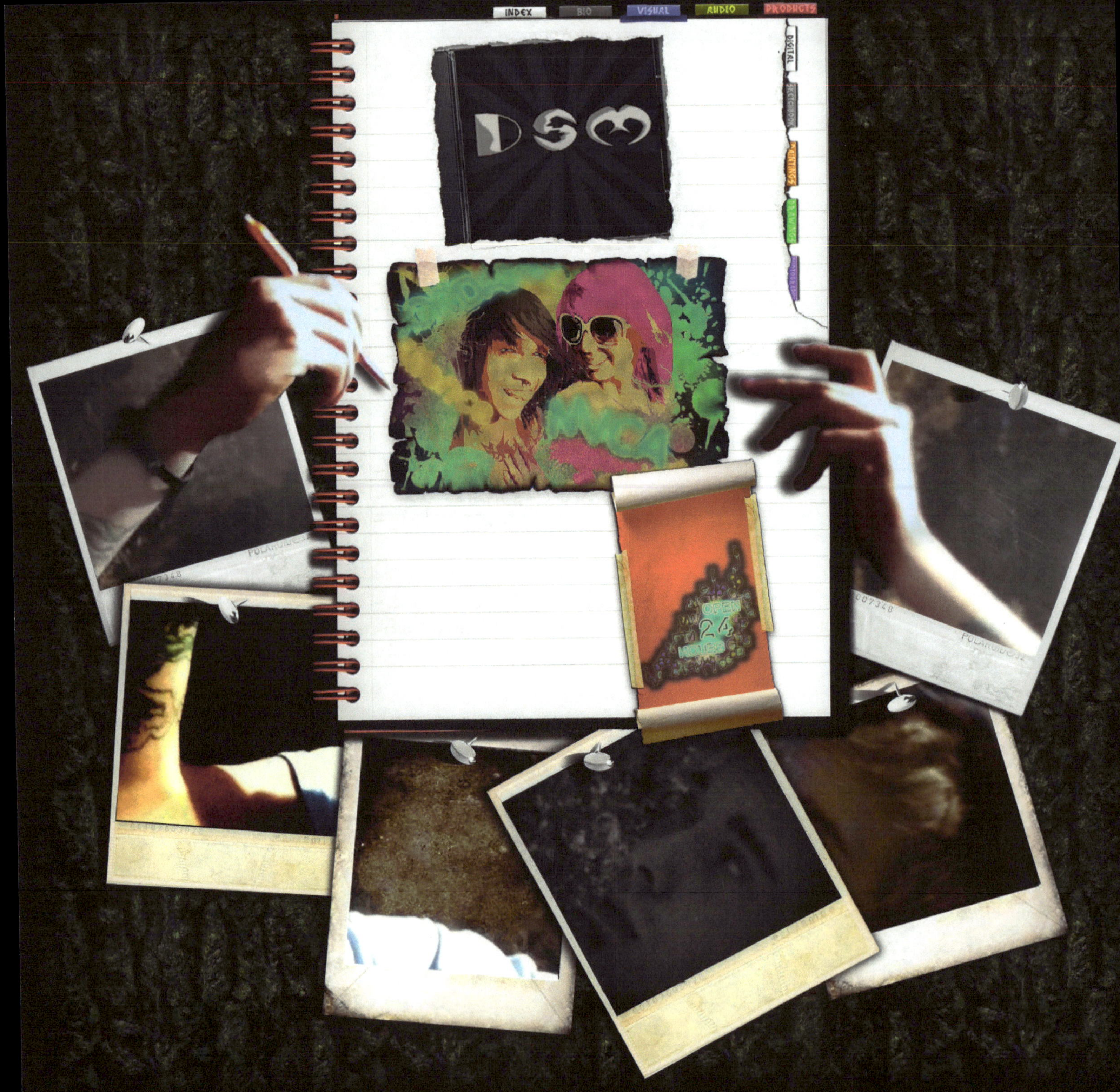
INDEX
BIO
VISUAL
AUDIO
PRODUCTS
DSM
DIGITAL
SKETCHBOOK
PAINTINGS
DRAWINGS
OPEN 24 HOURS
POLAROID

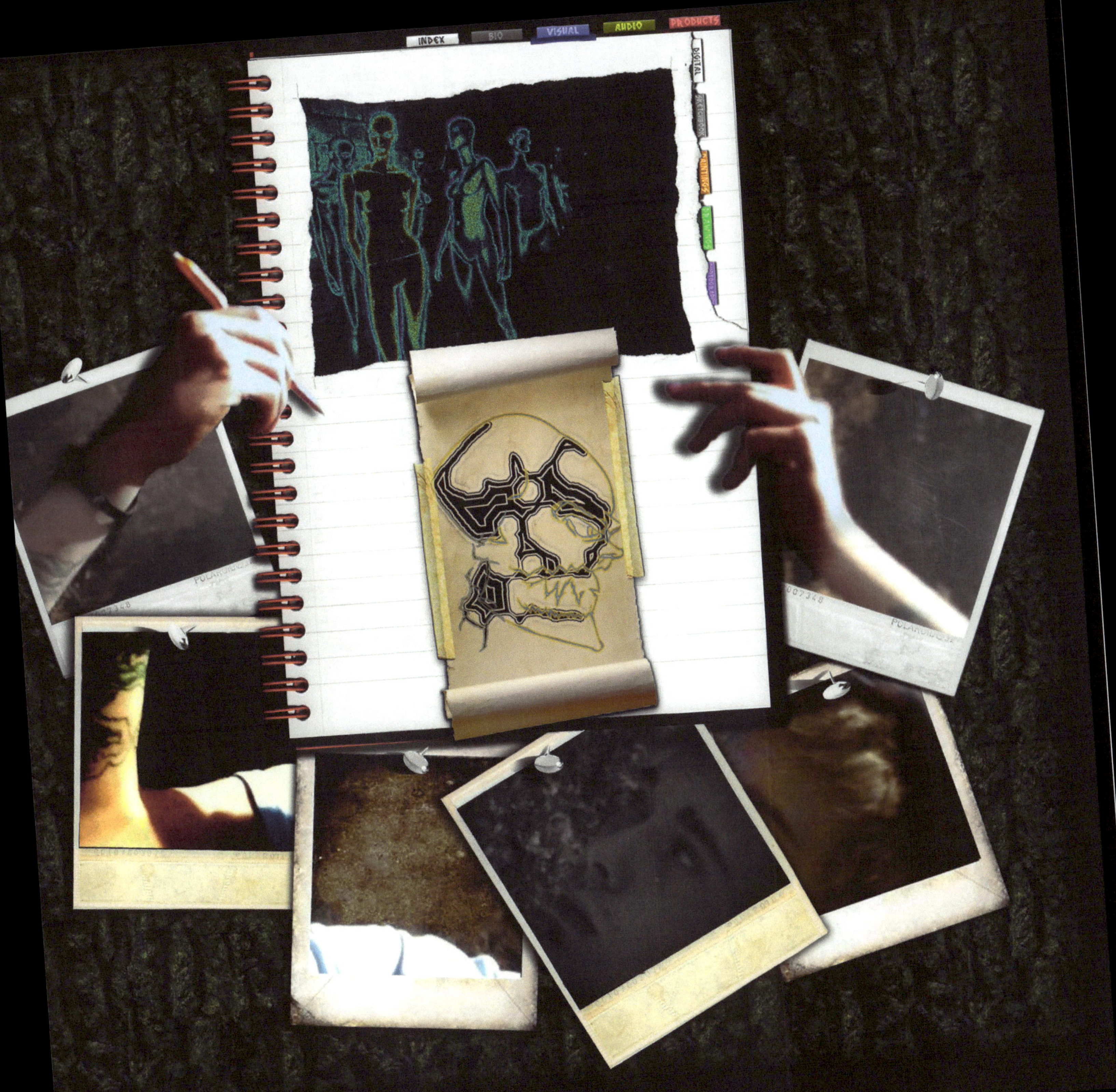

INDEX
BIO
VISUAL
AUDIO
PRODUCTS
DIGITAL
SKETCHBOOK
PAINTINGS
POLAROIDS

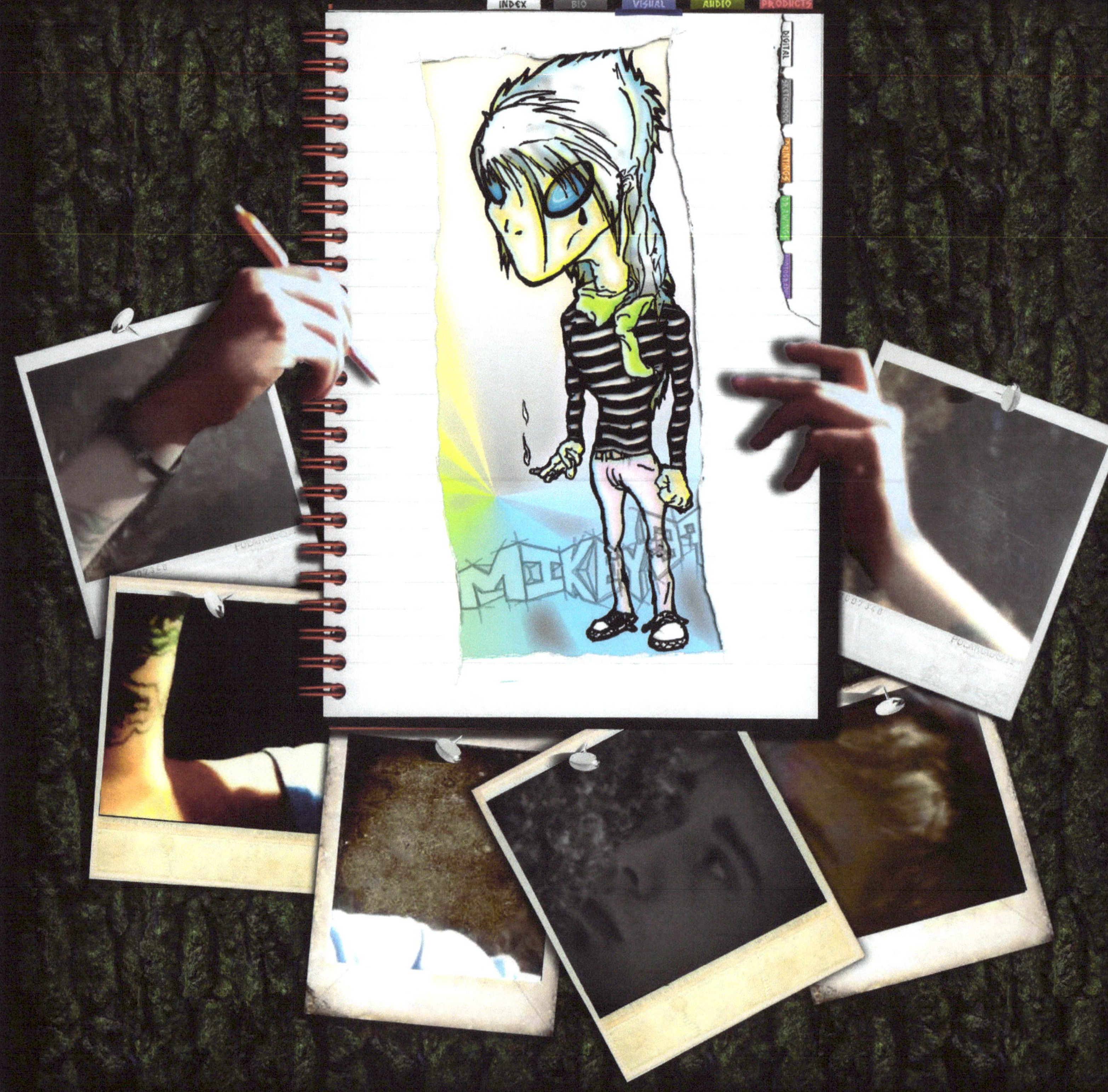

INDEX   BIO   VISUAL   AUDIO   PRODUCTS
DIGITAL
SKETCHBOOK
PAINTINGS

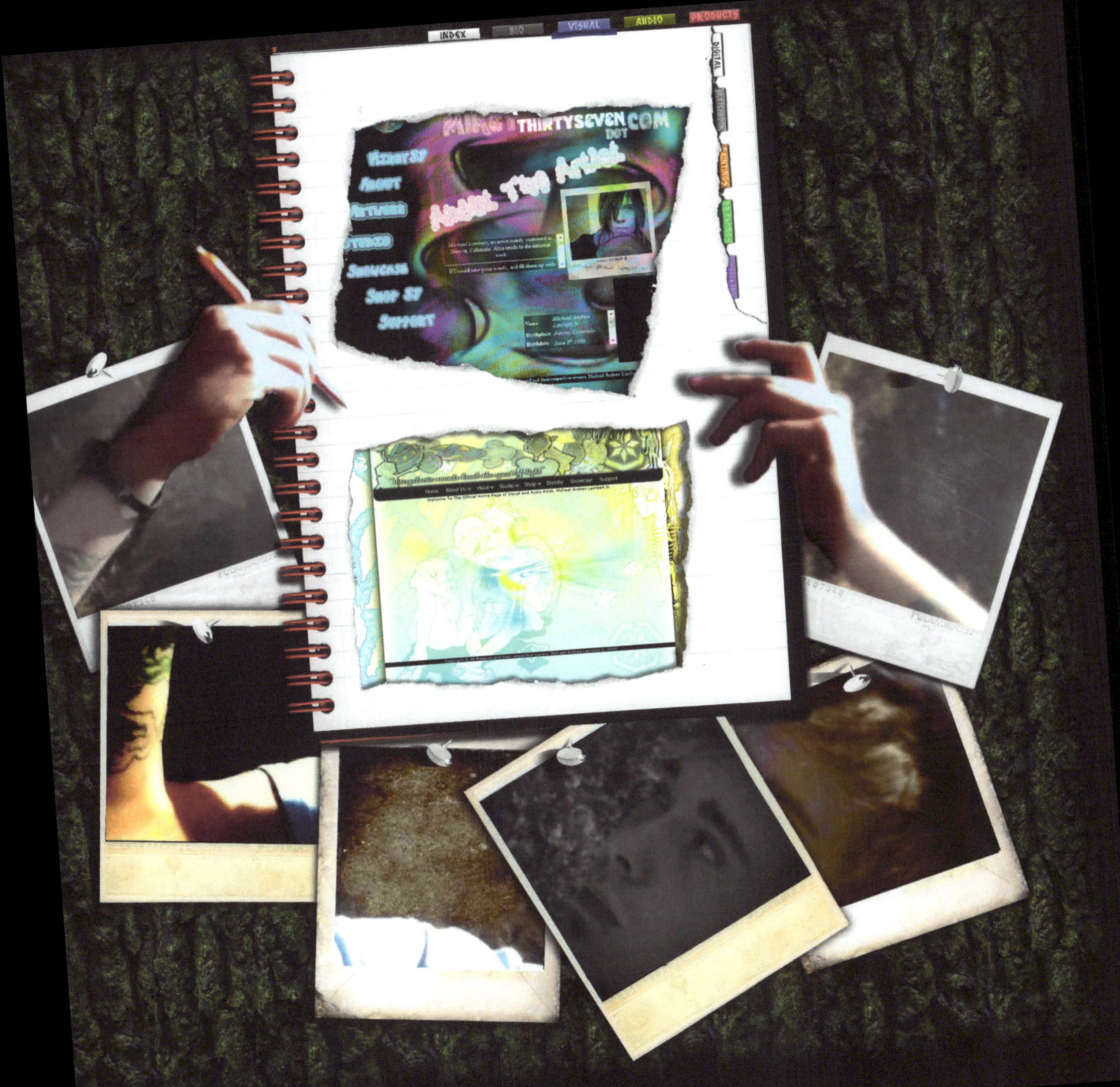
MIKEYTHIRTYSEVEN.COM DOT
MIKEY 37
ABOUT
ARTWORK
STUDIO
SHOWCASE
SHOP 37
SUPPORT
About The Artist
Michael Lambert, an artist mainly stationed in Denver, Colorado. Also tends to do national work.
MT would take your words, and fill them up with
Name   Michael Andrew Lambert Jr
Birthplace   Aurora, Colorado
Birthdate   June 1st 1990
DIGITAL
SKETCHBOOK
PAINTINGS
Home   About Us   Visual   Studio   Shop   Divinity   Showcase   Support
Welcome To The Official Home Page of Visual and Audio Artist, Michael Andrew Lambert Jr.
Copyright © All Material and their respective owners. Michael Andrew Lambert Jr. 2010
INDEX   BIO   VISUAL   AUDIO   PRODUCTS

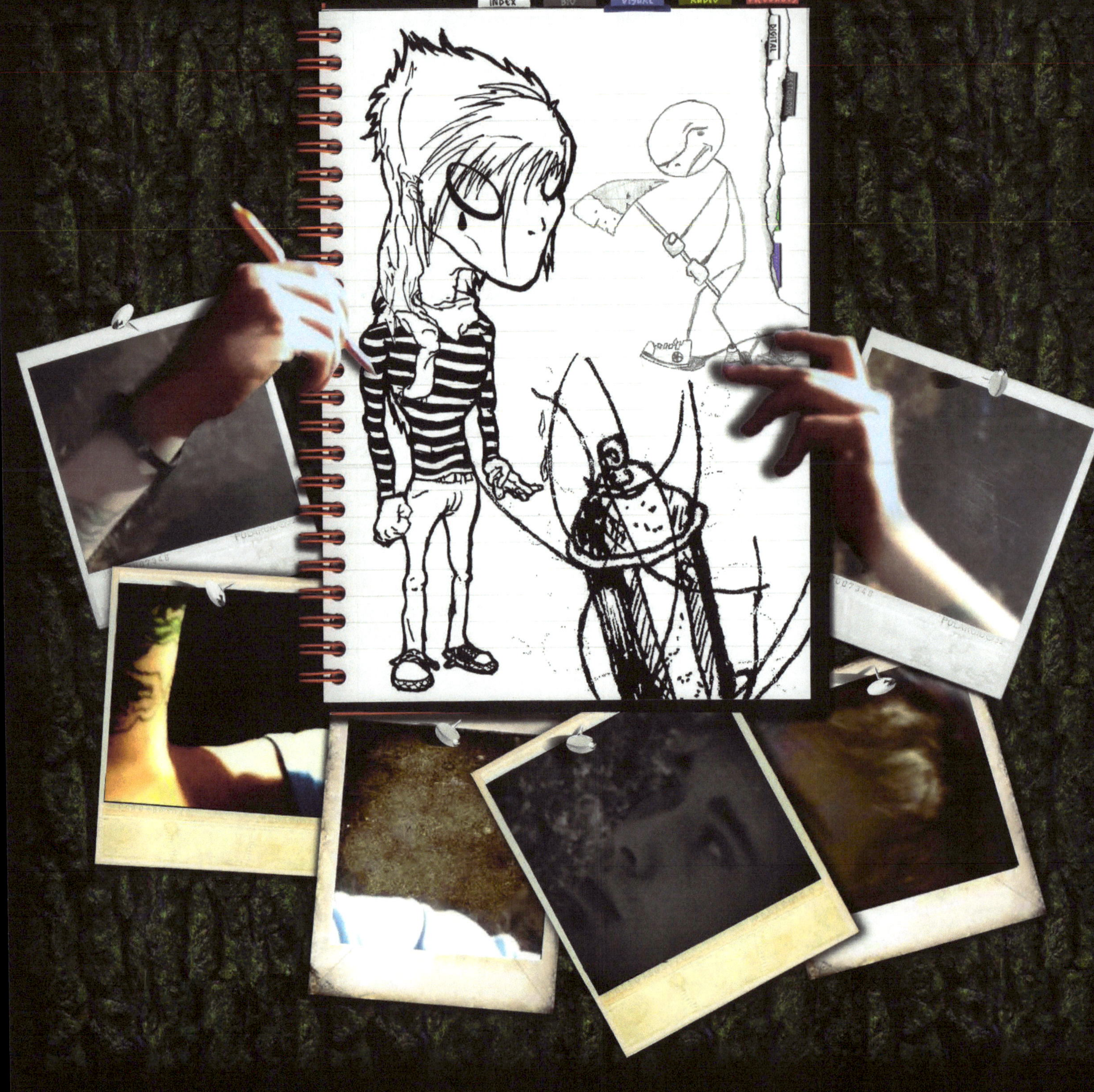
DIGITAL

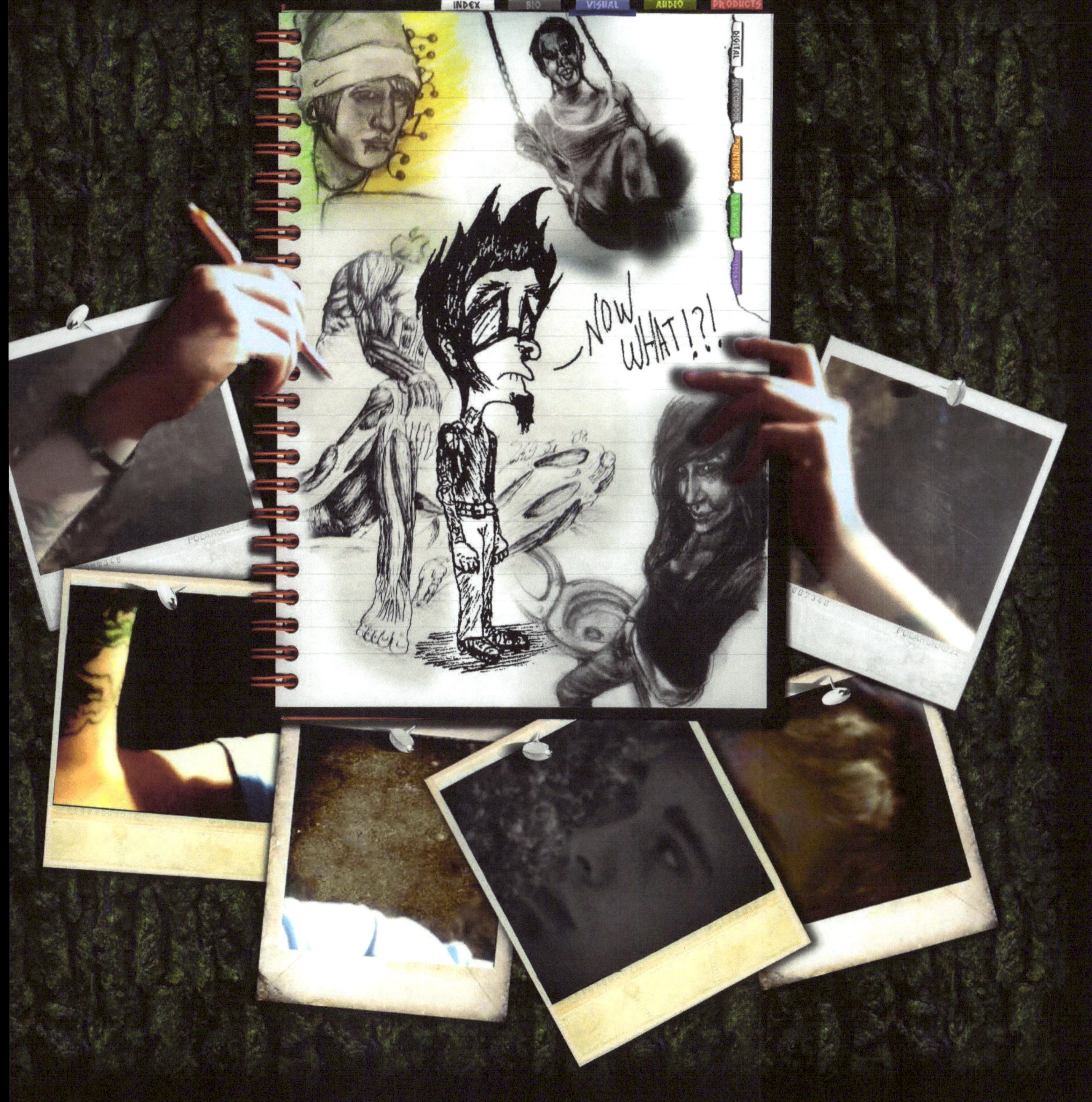
INDEX
BIO
VISUAL
AUDIO
PRODUCTS
DIGITAL
SKETCHBOOK
PAINTINGS
DRAWINGS
NOW WHAT!?!

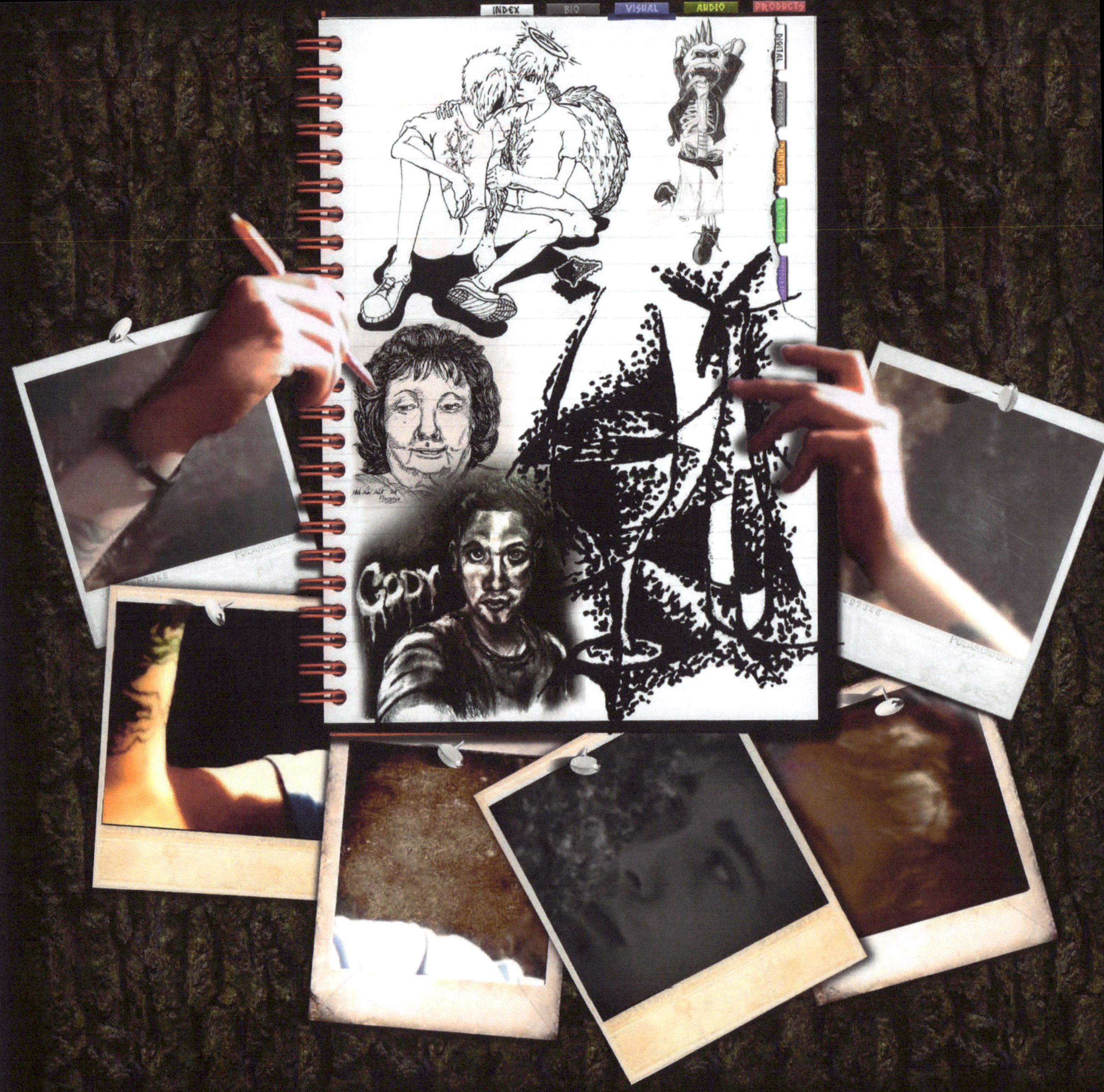
INDEX
BIO
VISUAL
AUDIO
PRODUCTS
DIGITAL
SKETCHBOOK
PAINTINGS
GRAPHICS
CODY

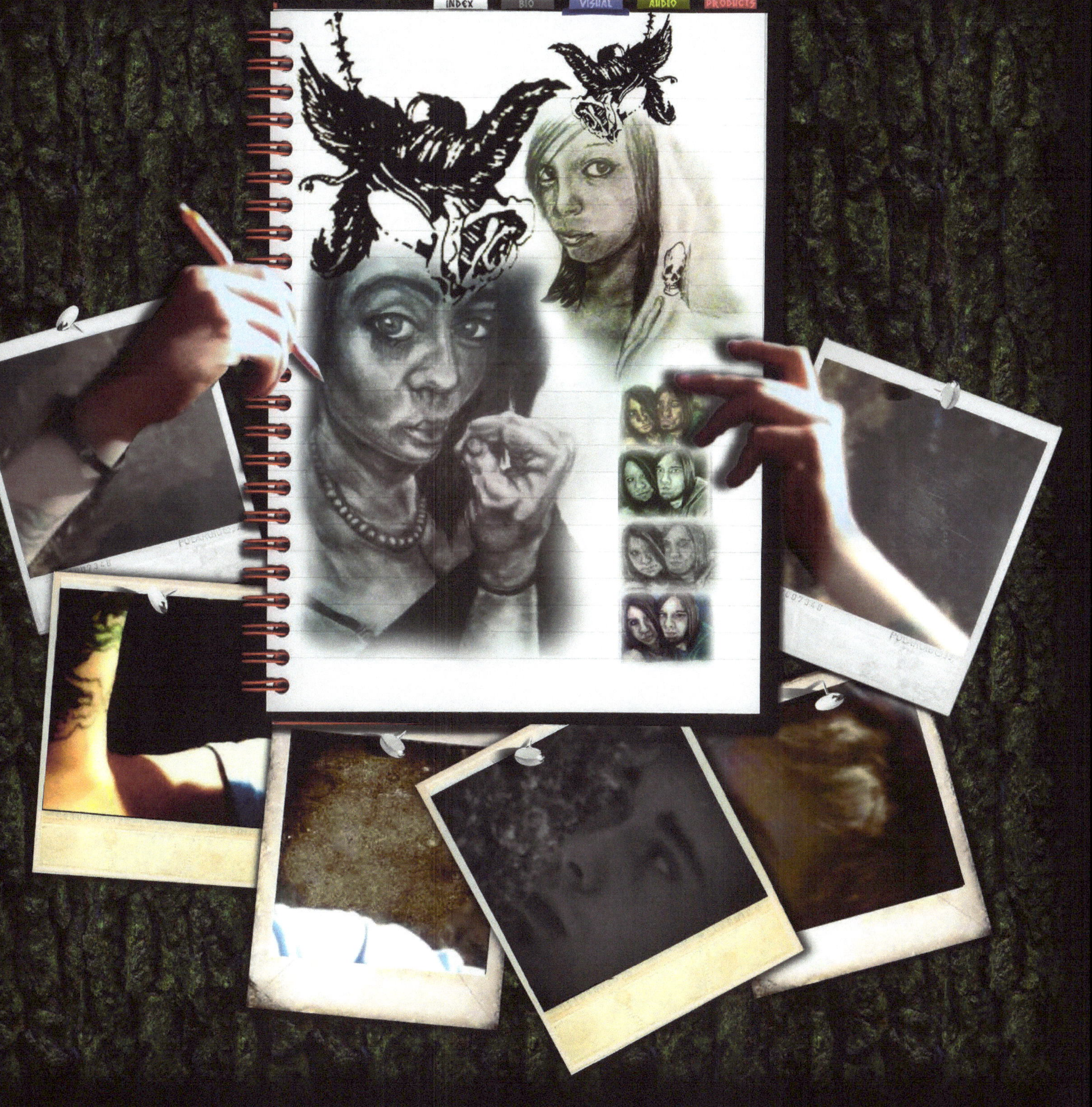

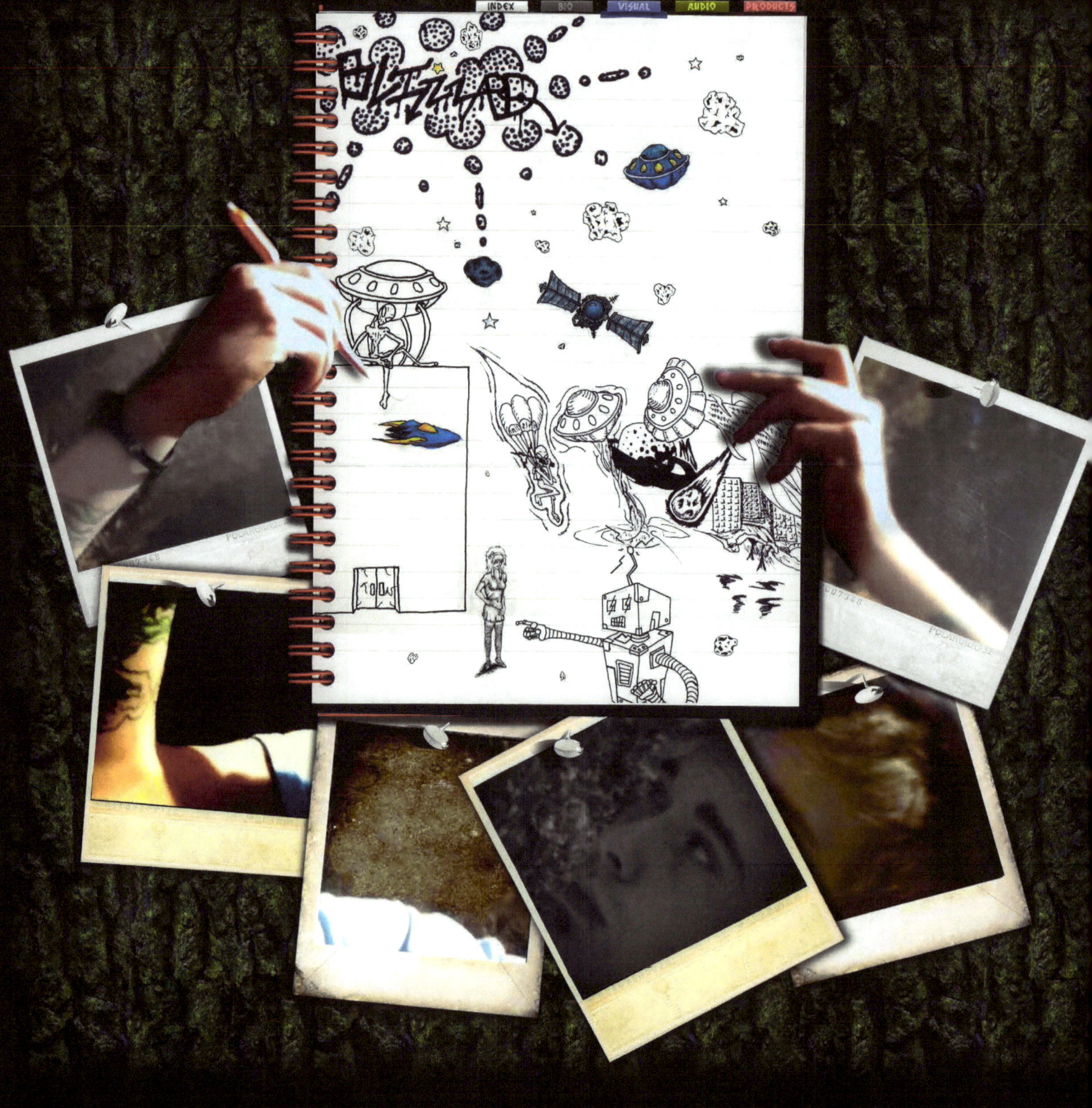

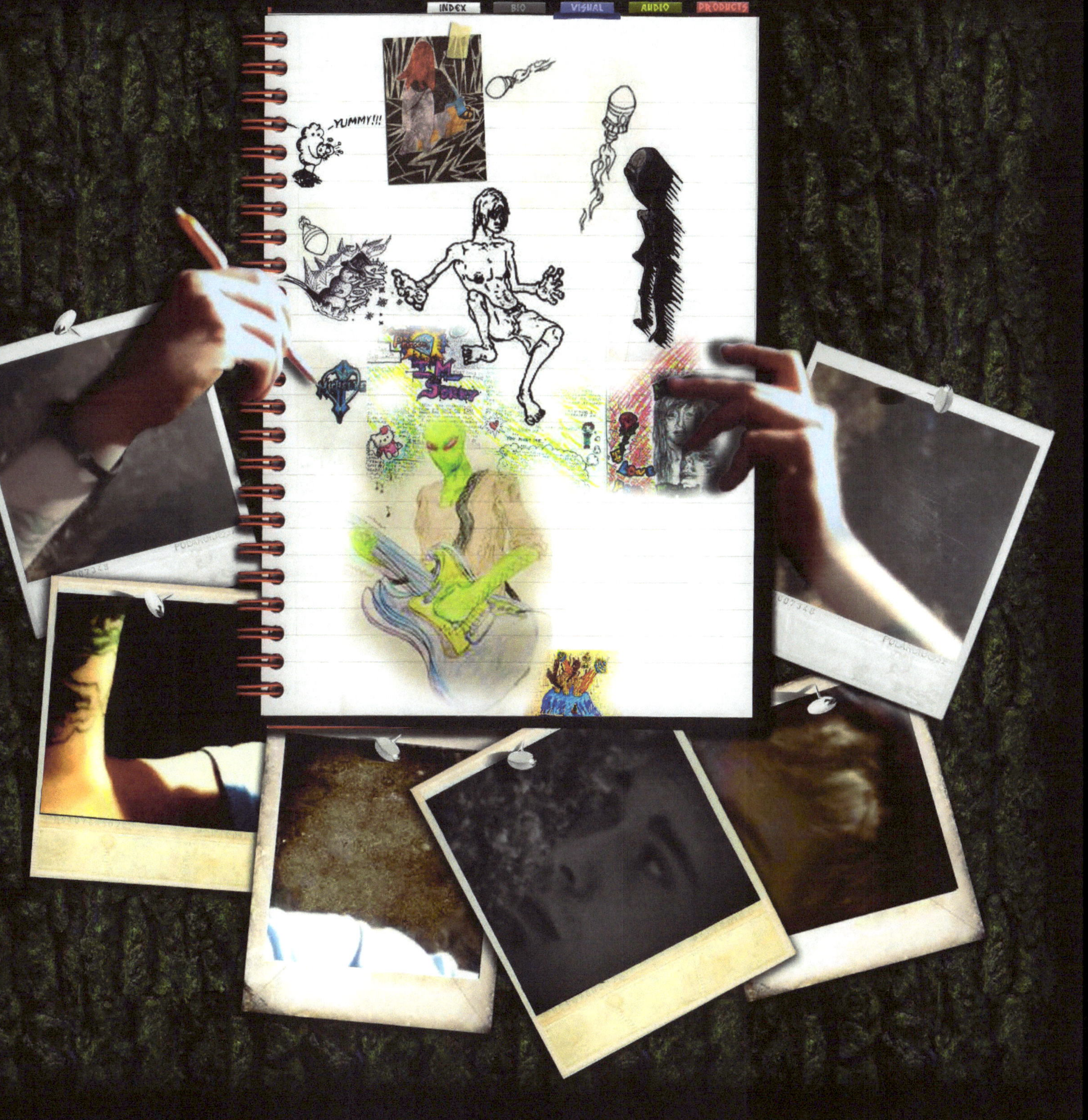
-YUMMY!!!

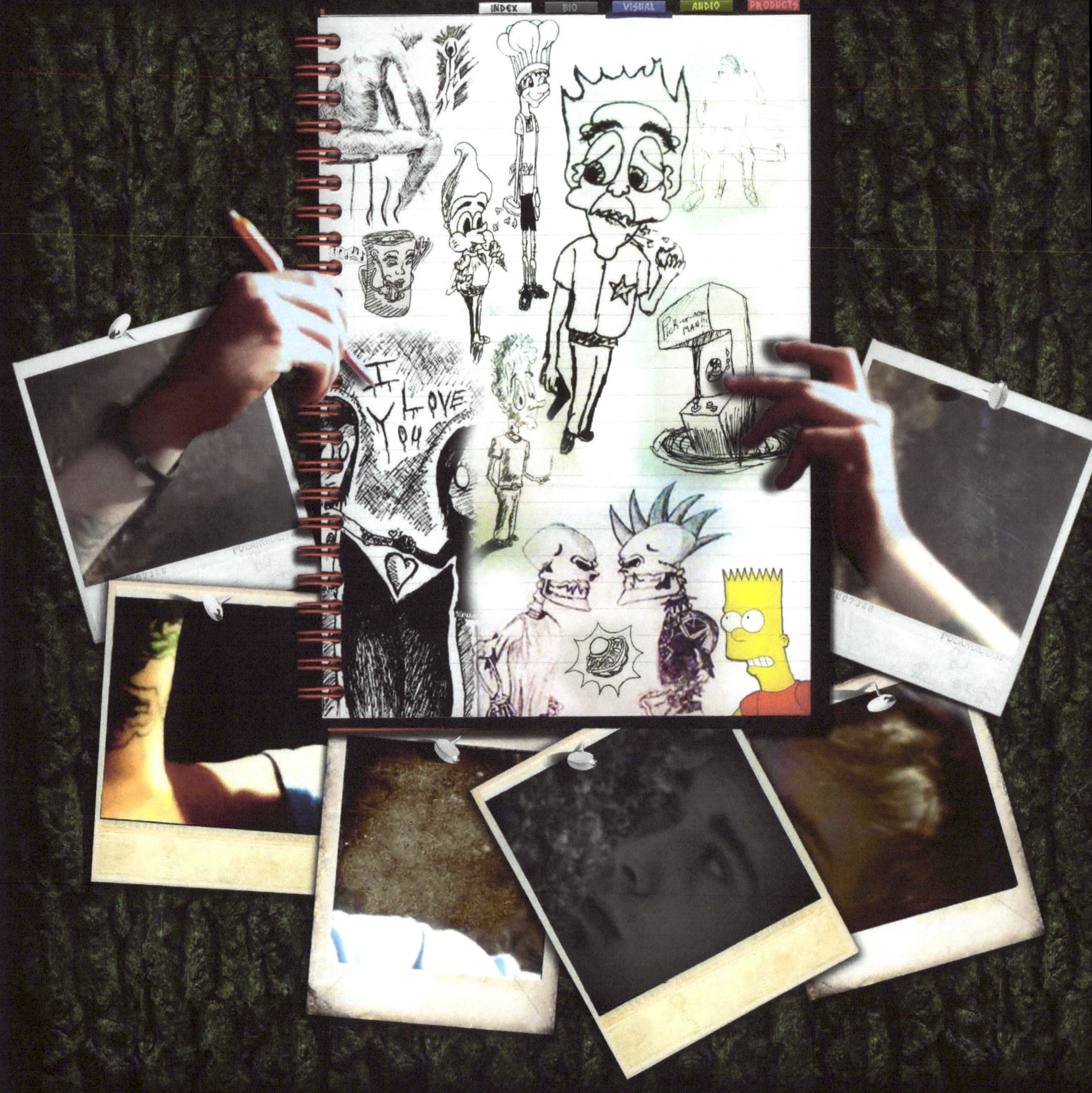
I LOVE YOU
Pick-ur-nox
MAN !!!

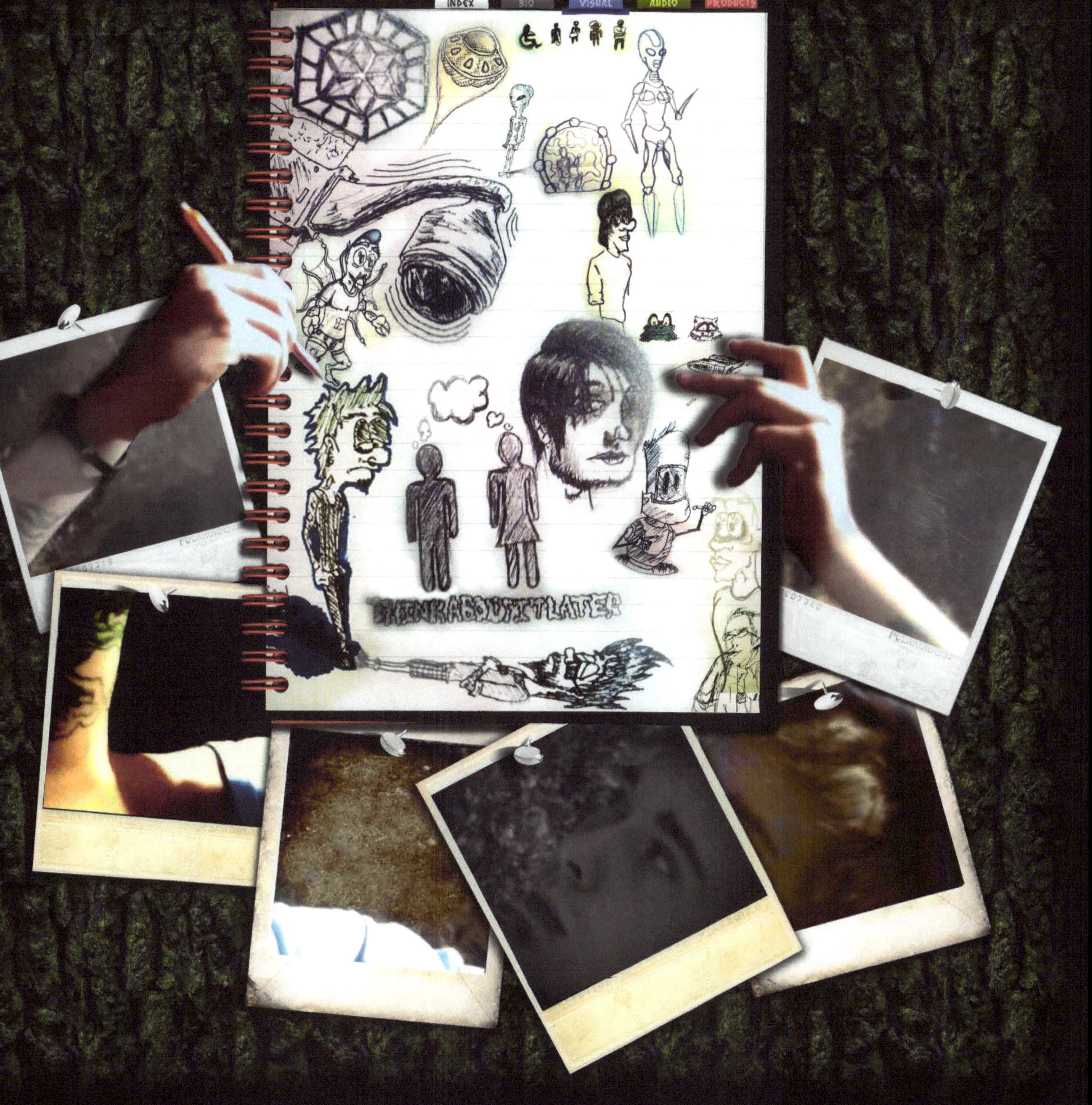
THINKABOUTITLATER

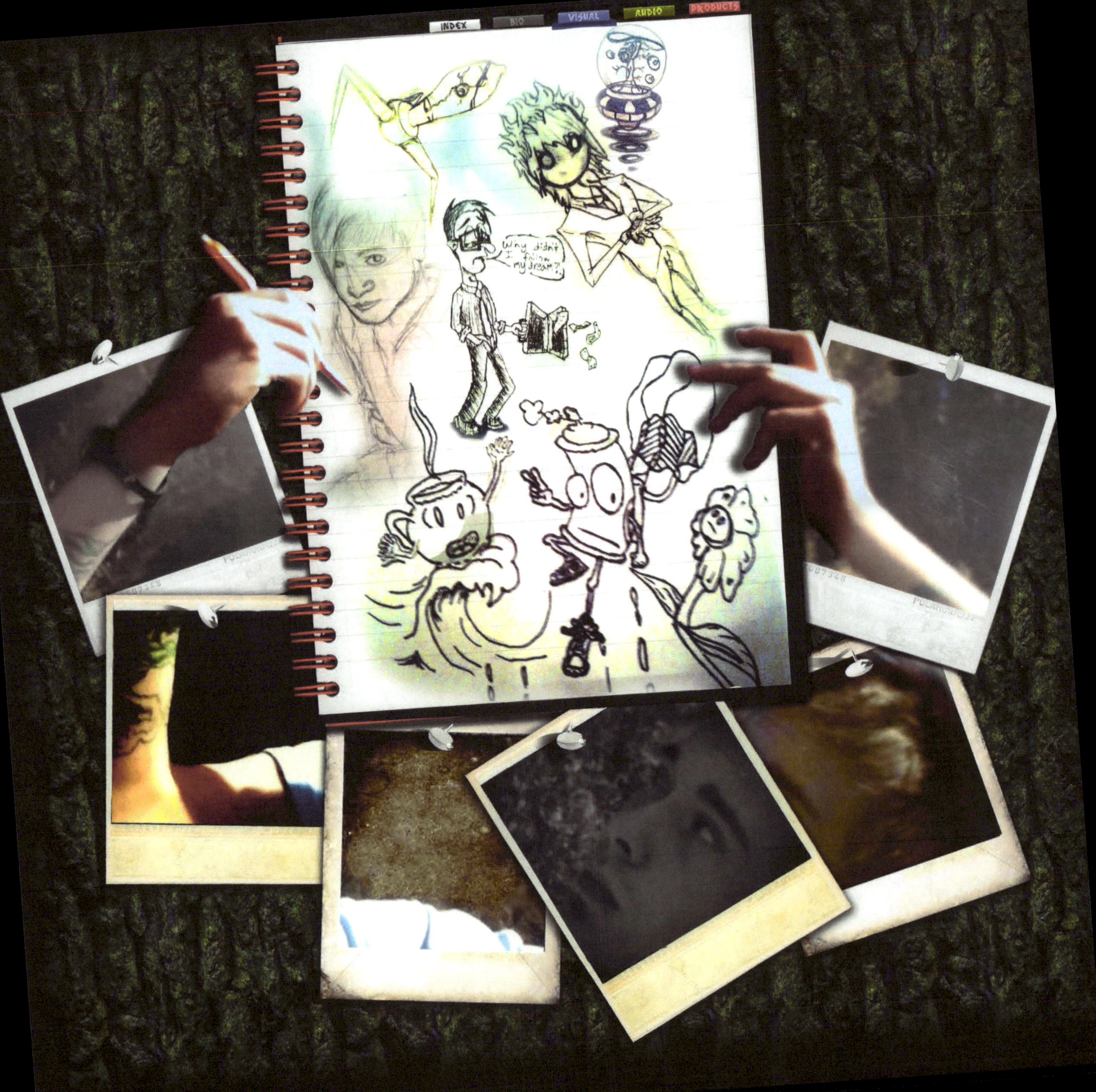
Why didn't I follow my dream?

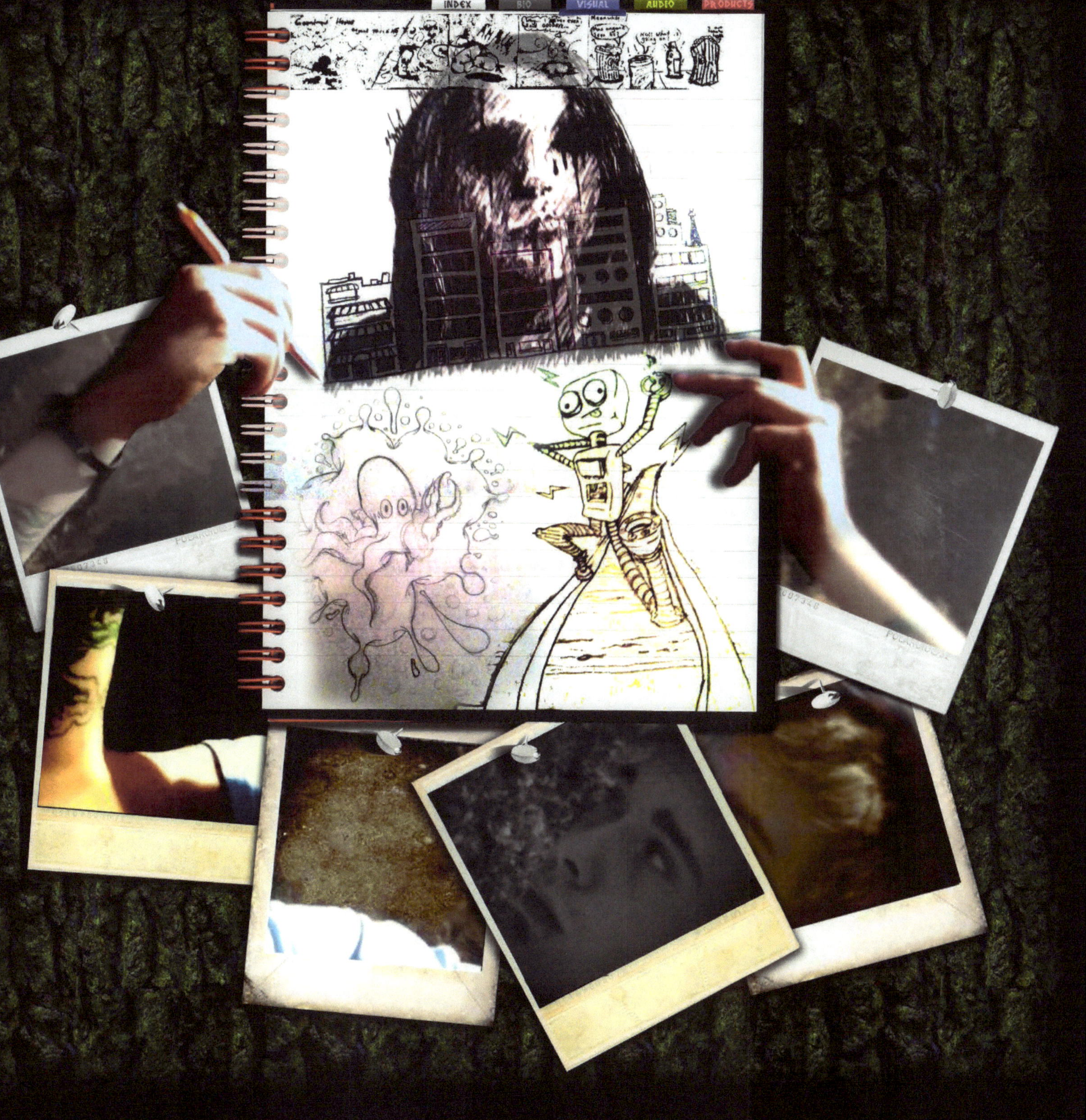

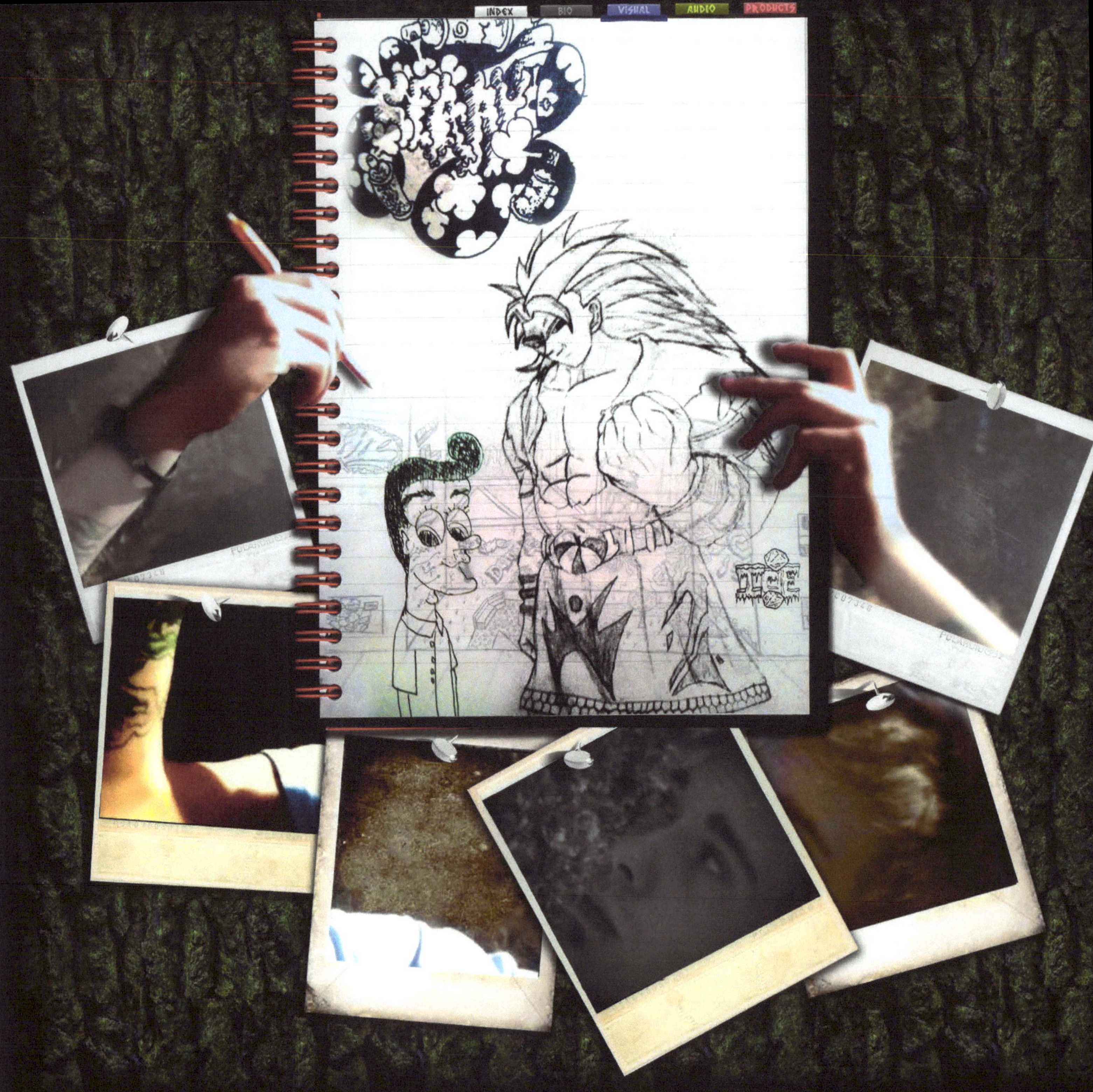

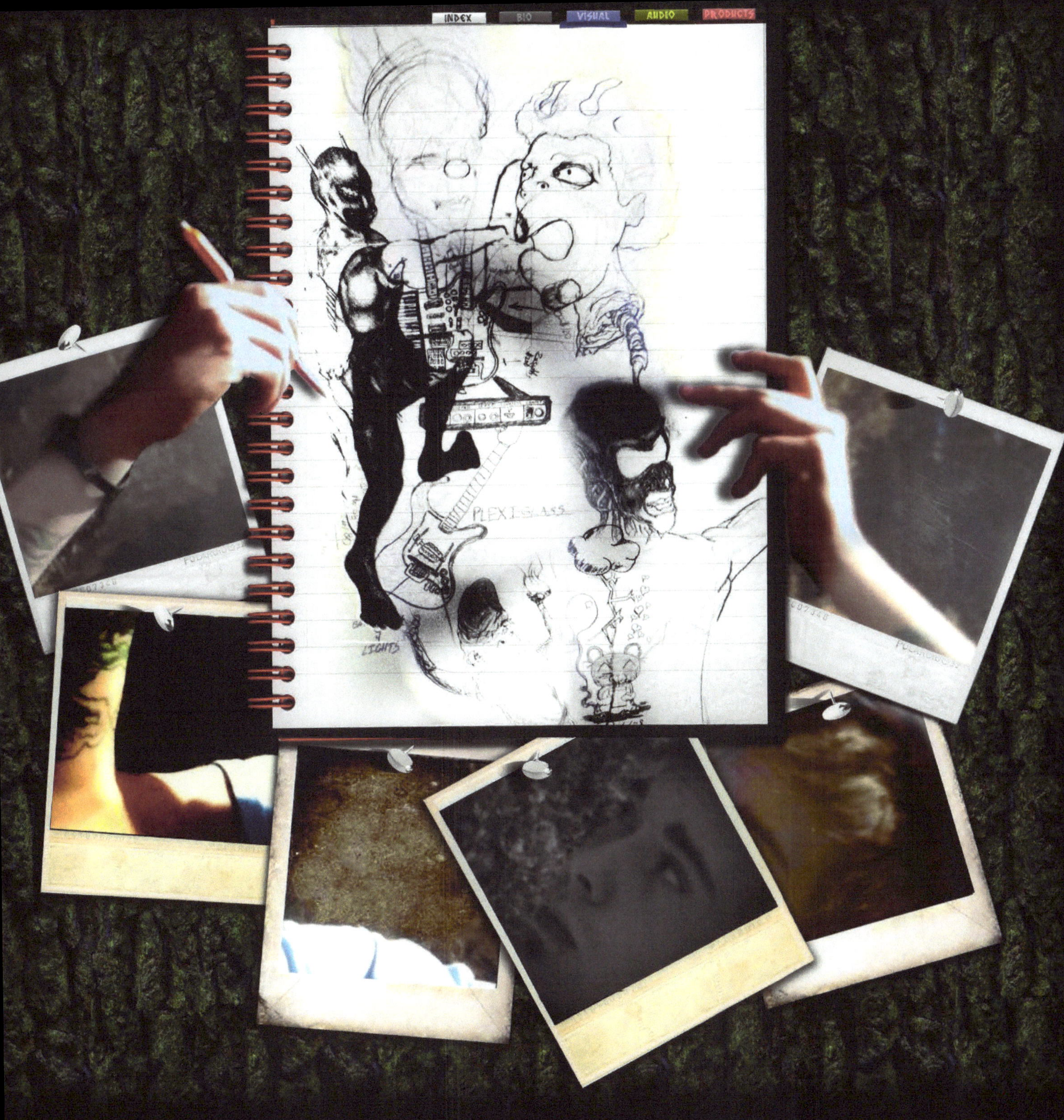
PLEXIGLASS
LIGHTS

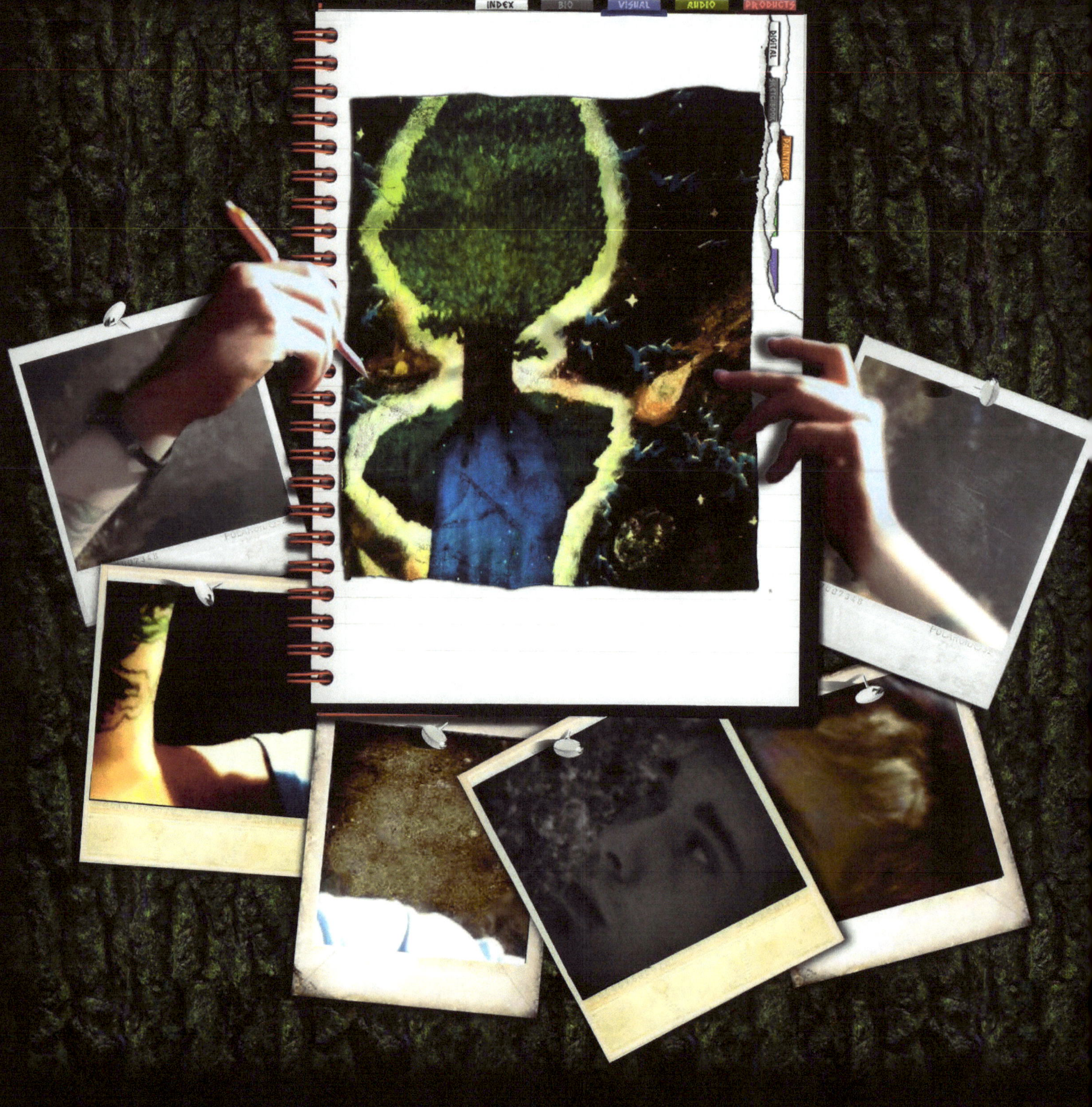

INDEX
BIO
VISUAL
AUDIO
PRODUCTS
DIGITAL
PAINTINGS

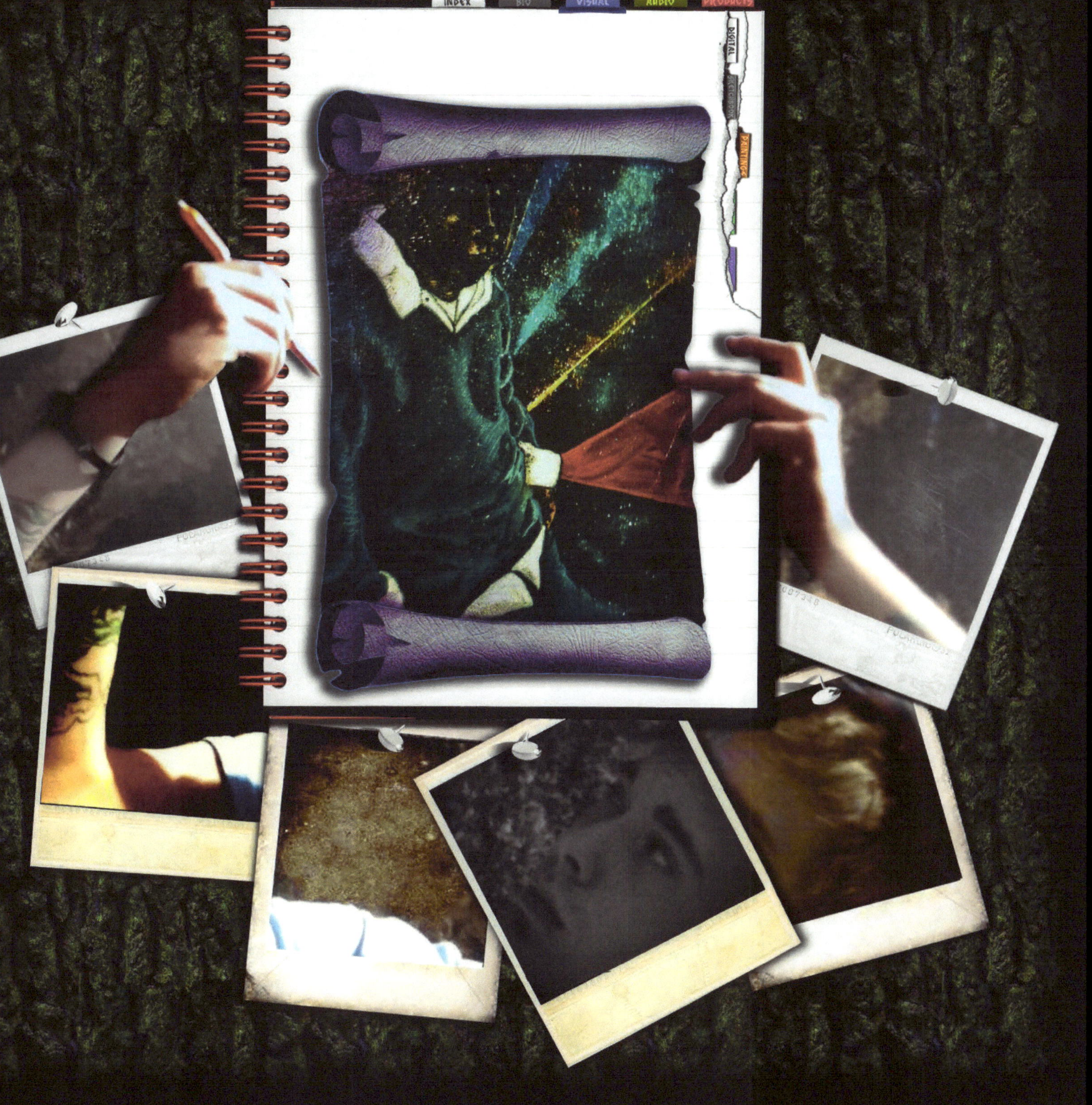
INDEX
BIO
VISUAL
AUDIO
PRODUCTS
DIGITAL
PAINTINGS

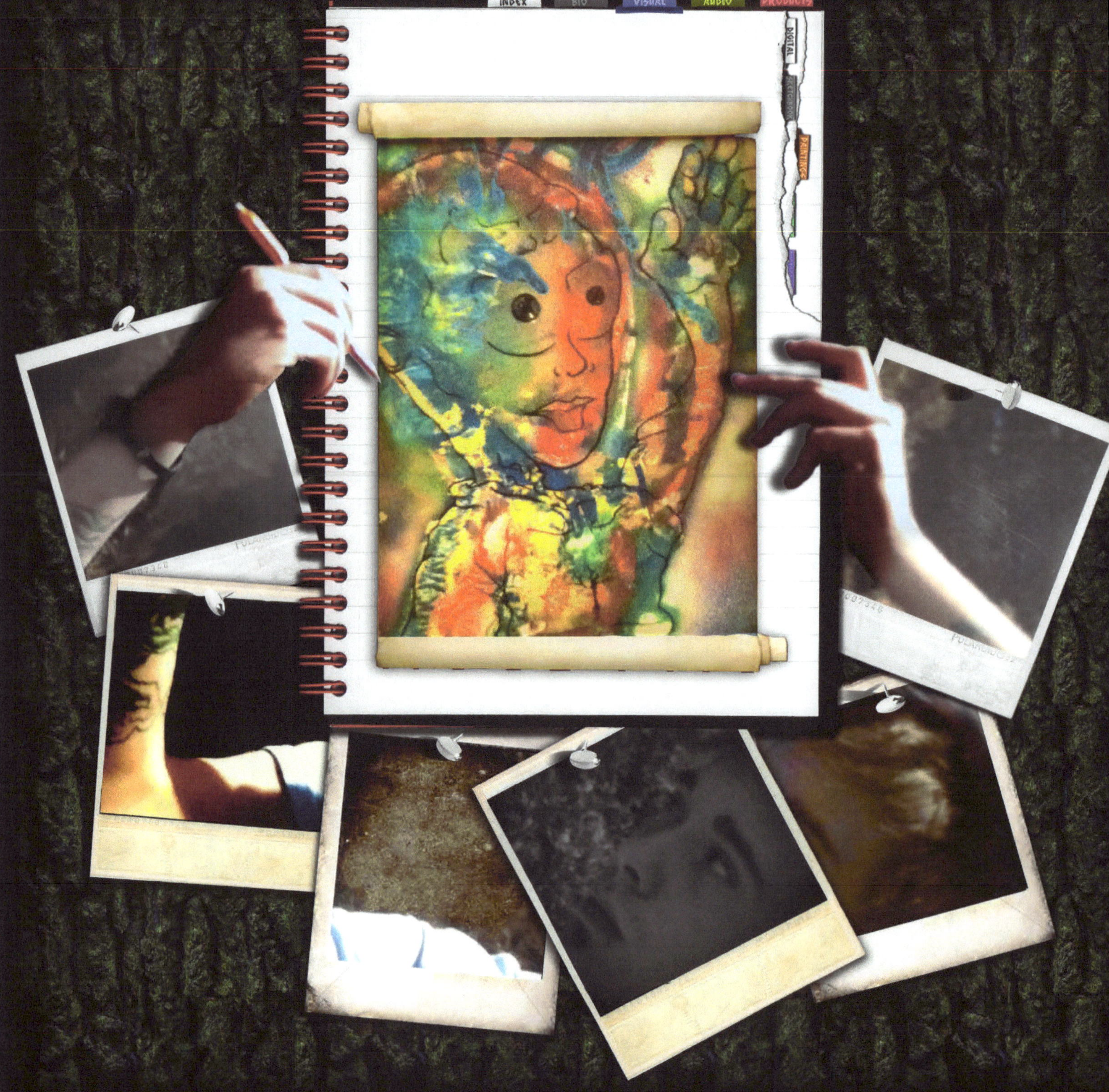

INDEX
BIO
VISUAL
AUDIO
PRODUCTS
DIGITAL
PAINTINGS

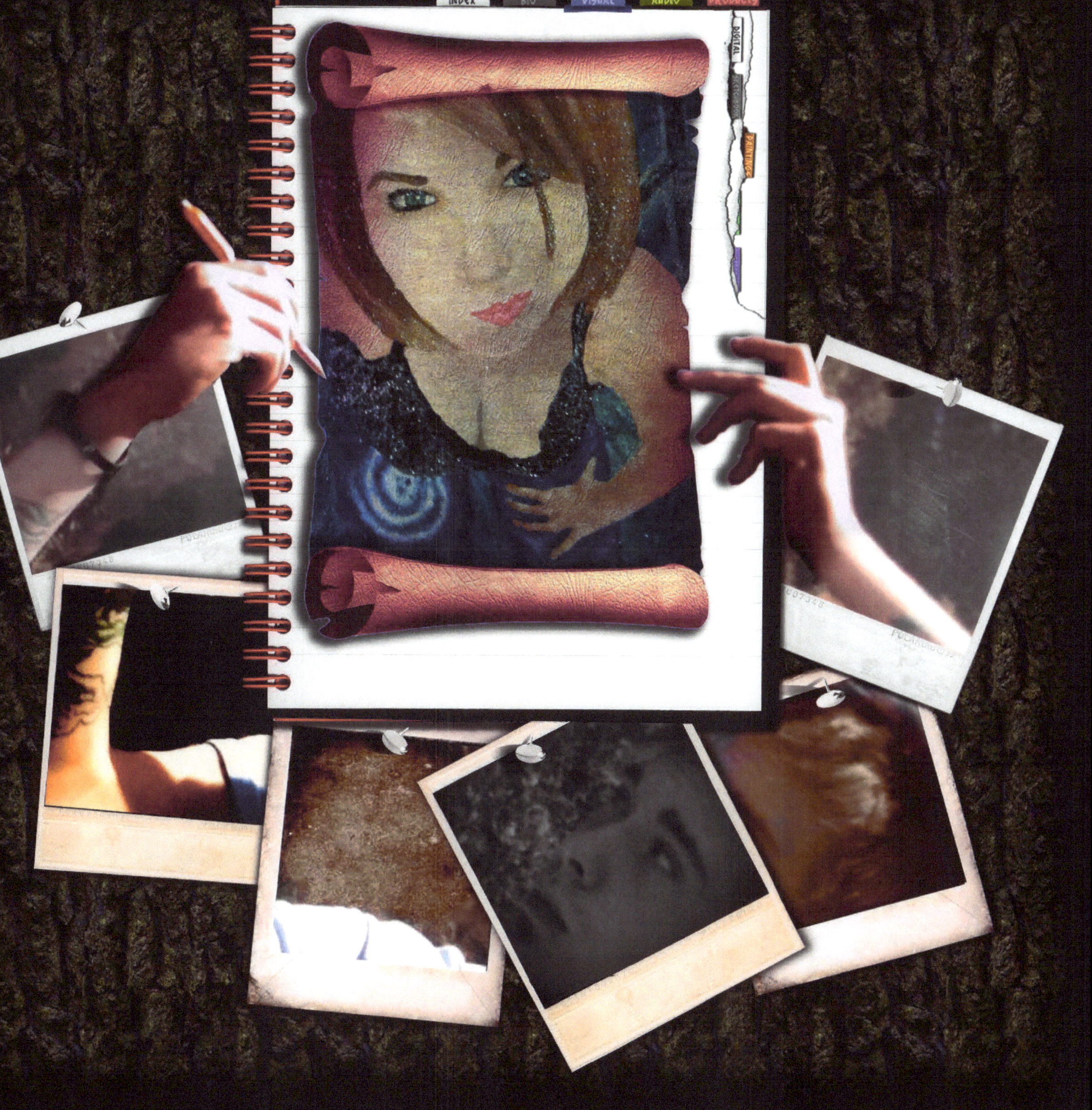

INDEX
BIO
VISUAL
AUDIO
PRODUCTS
DIGITAL
SKETCHBOOK
PAINTINGS

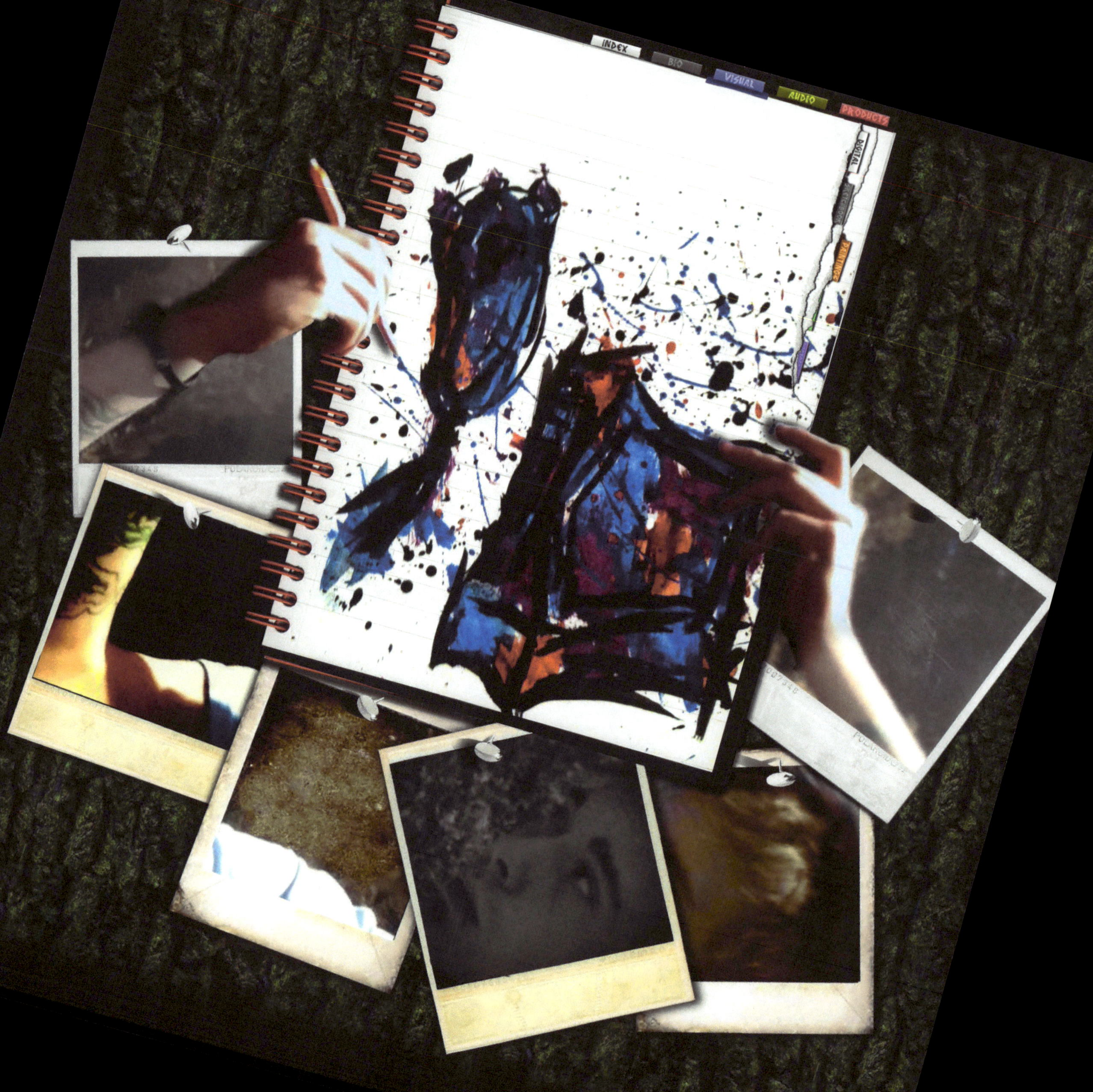
INDEX
BIO
VISUAL
AUDIO
PRODUCTS
DIGITAL
SCULPTURE
PAINTING

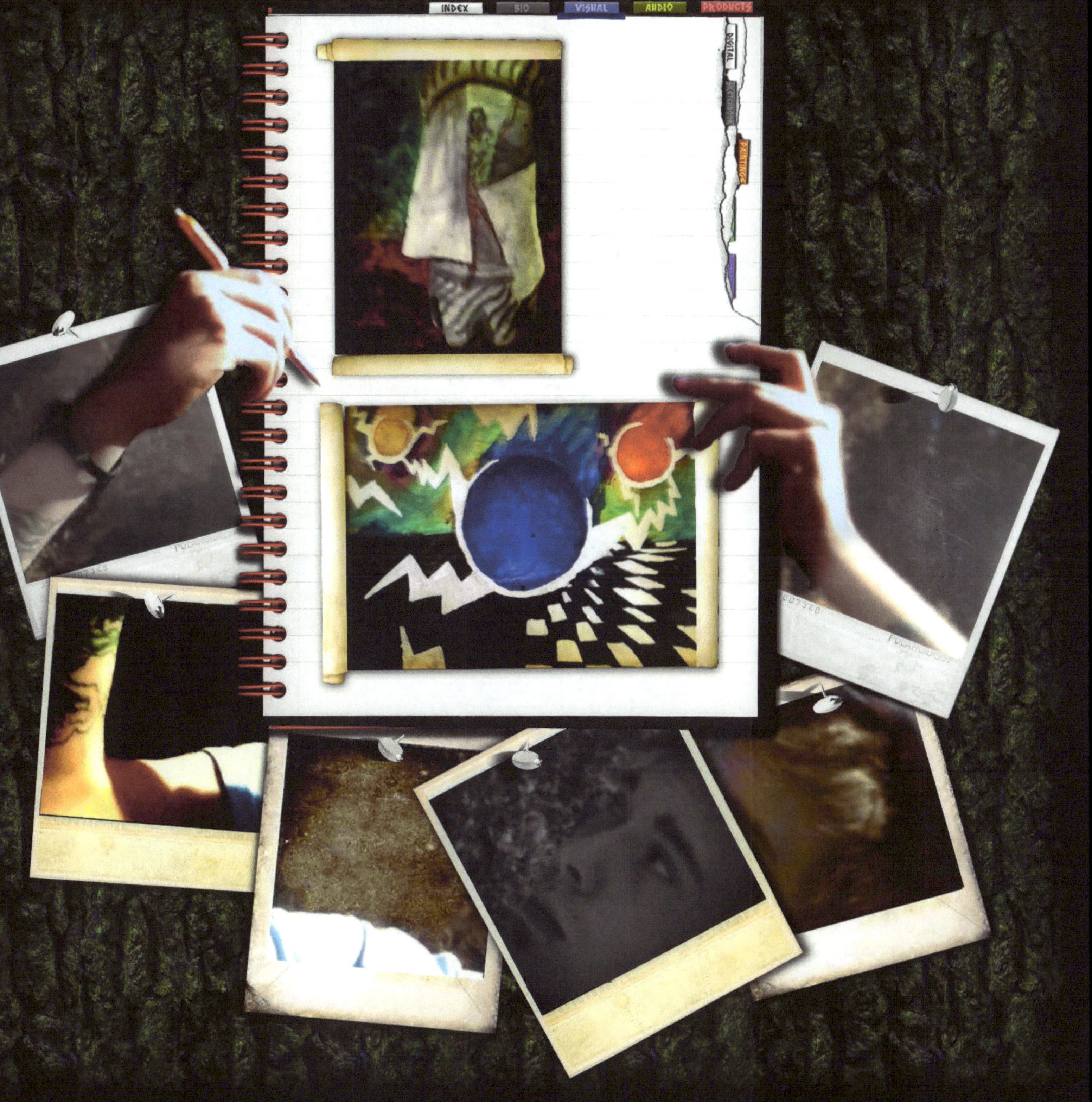

INDEX
BIO
VISUAL
AUDIO
PRODUCTS
DIGITAL
PAINTINGS

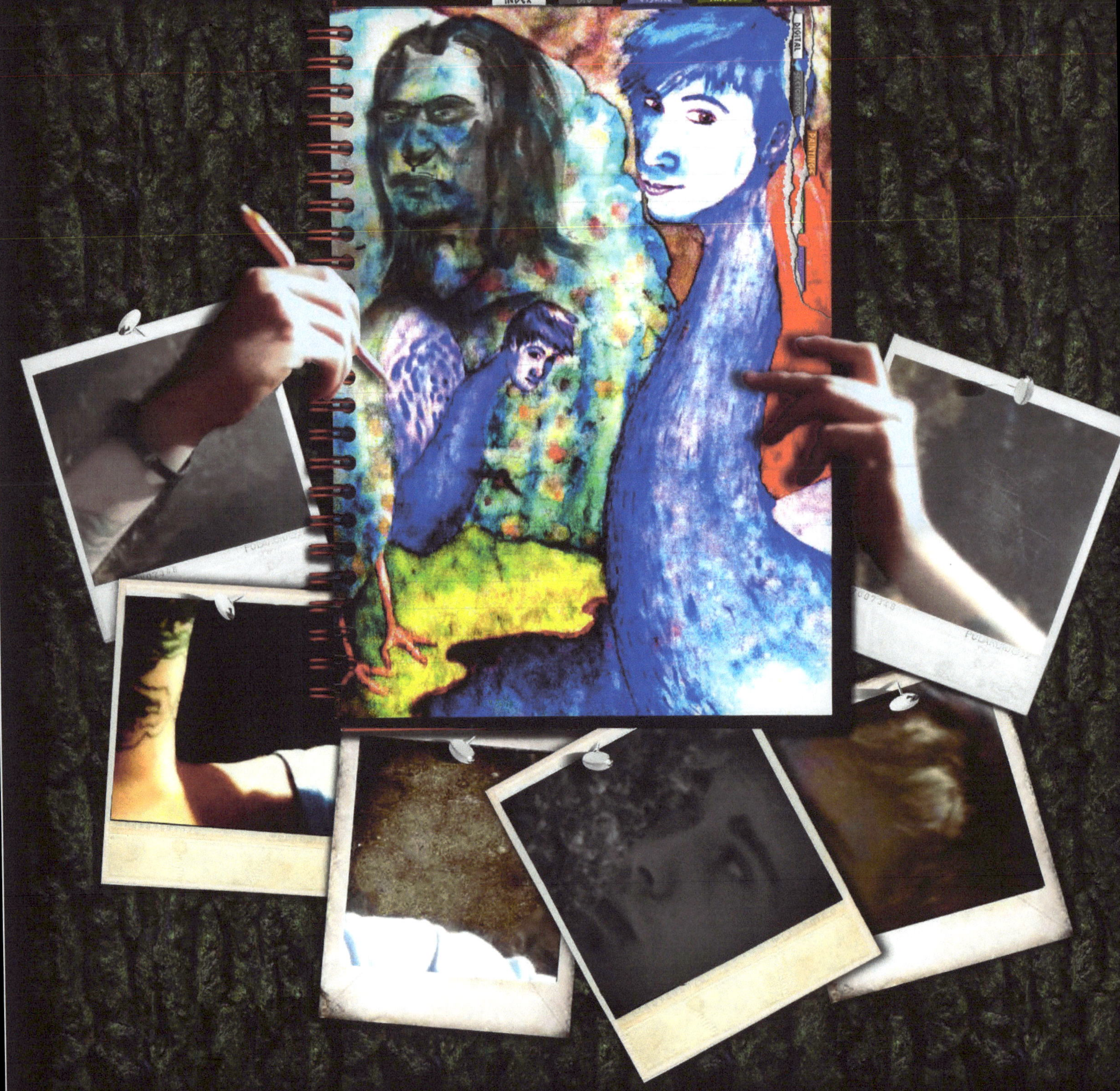

INDEX
BIO
VISUAL
AUDIO
PRODUCTS
DIGITAL
PAINTINGS

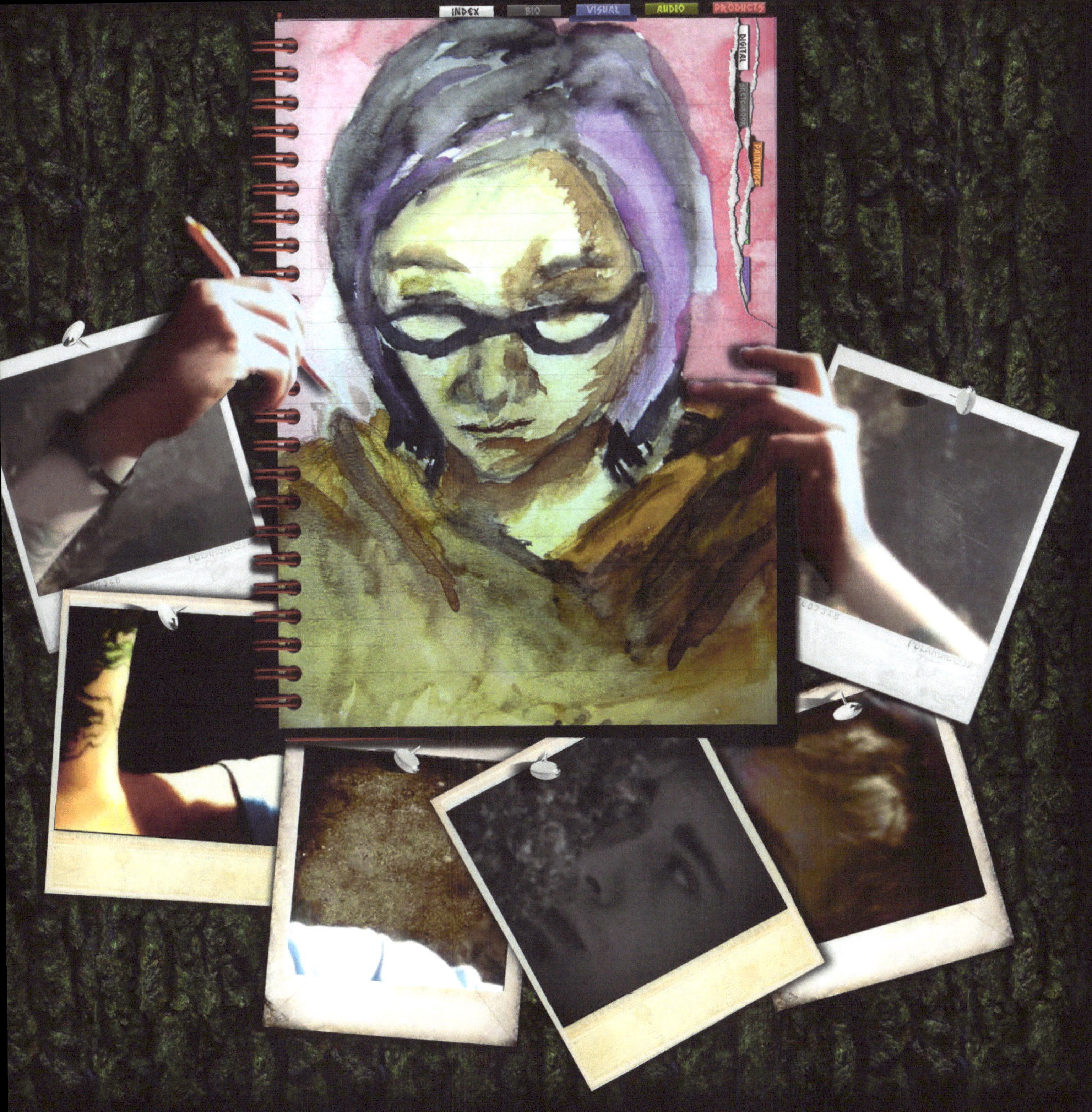

INDEX
BIO
VISUAL
AUDIO
PRODUCTS
DIGITAL
SKETCHBOOK
PAINTINGS

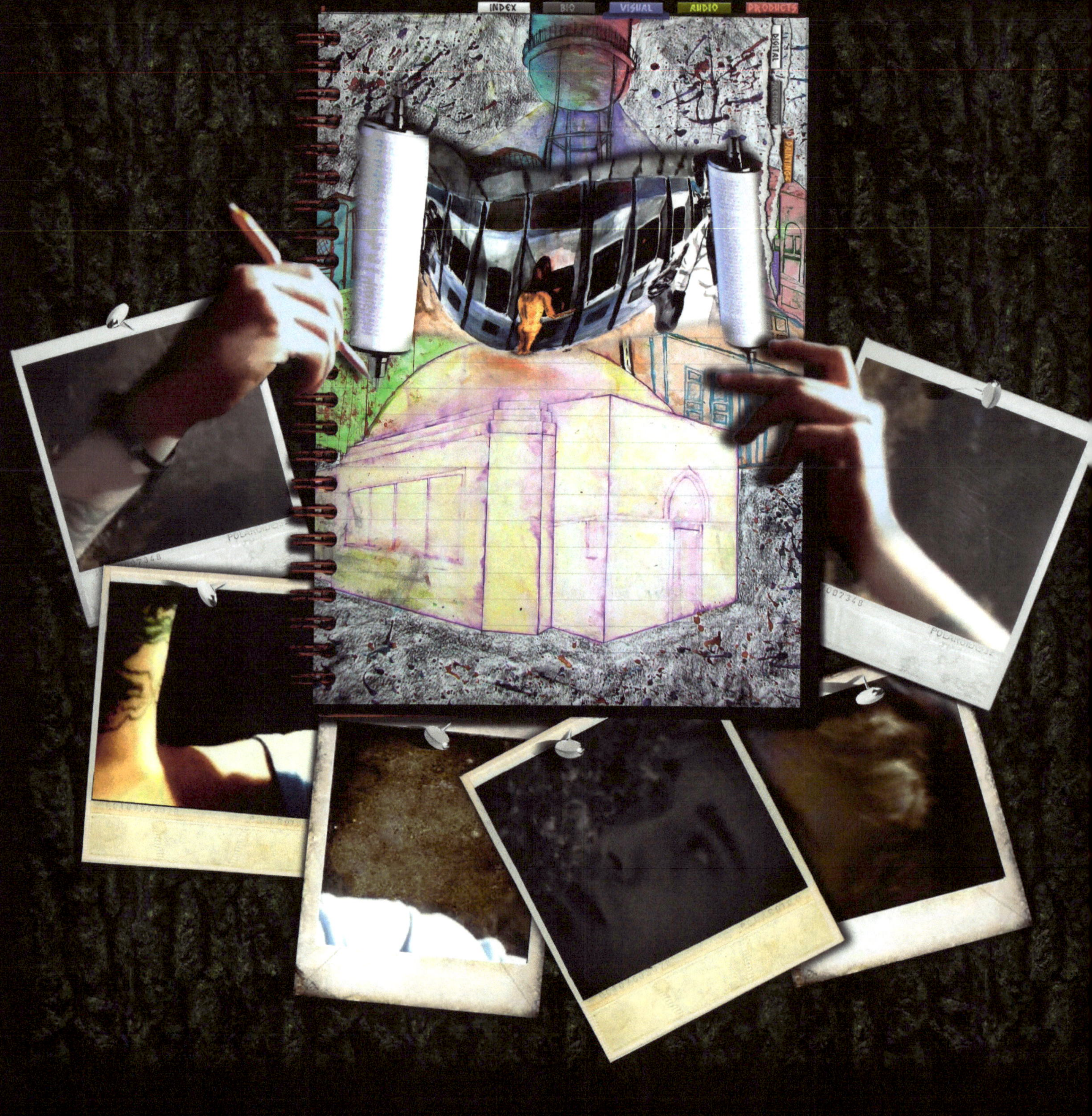

INDEX BIO VISUAL AUDIO PRODUCTS
DIGITAL
PAINTING

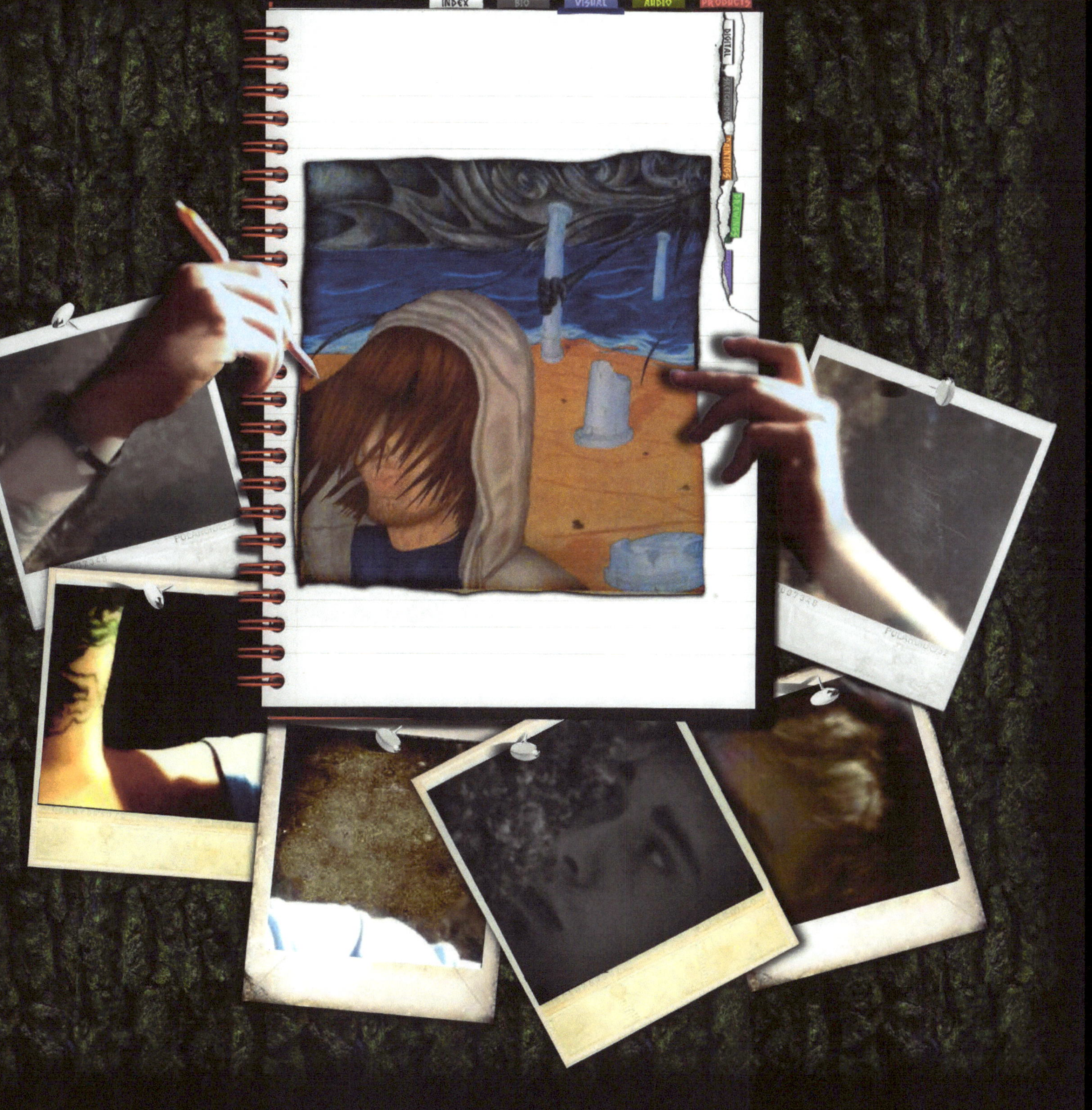

INDEX
BIO
VISUAL
AUDIO
PRODUCTS
DIGITAL
SKETCHBOOK
PAINTINGS
DRAWINGS

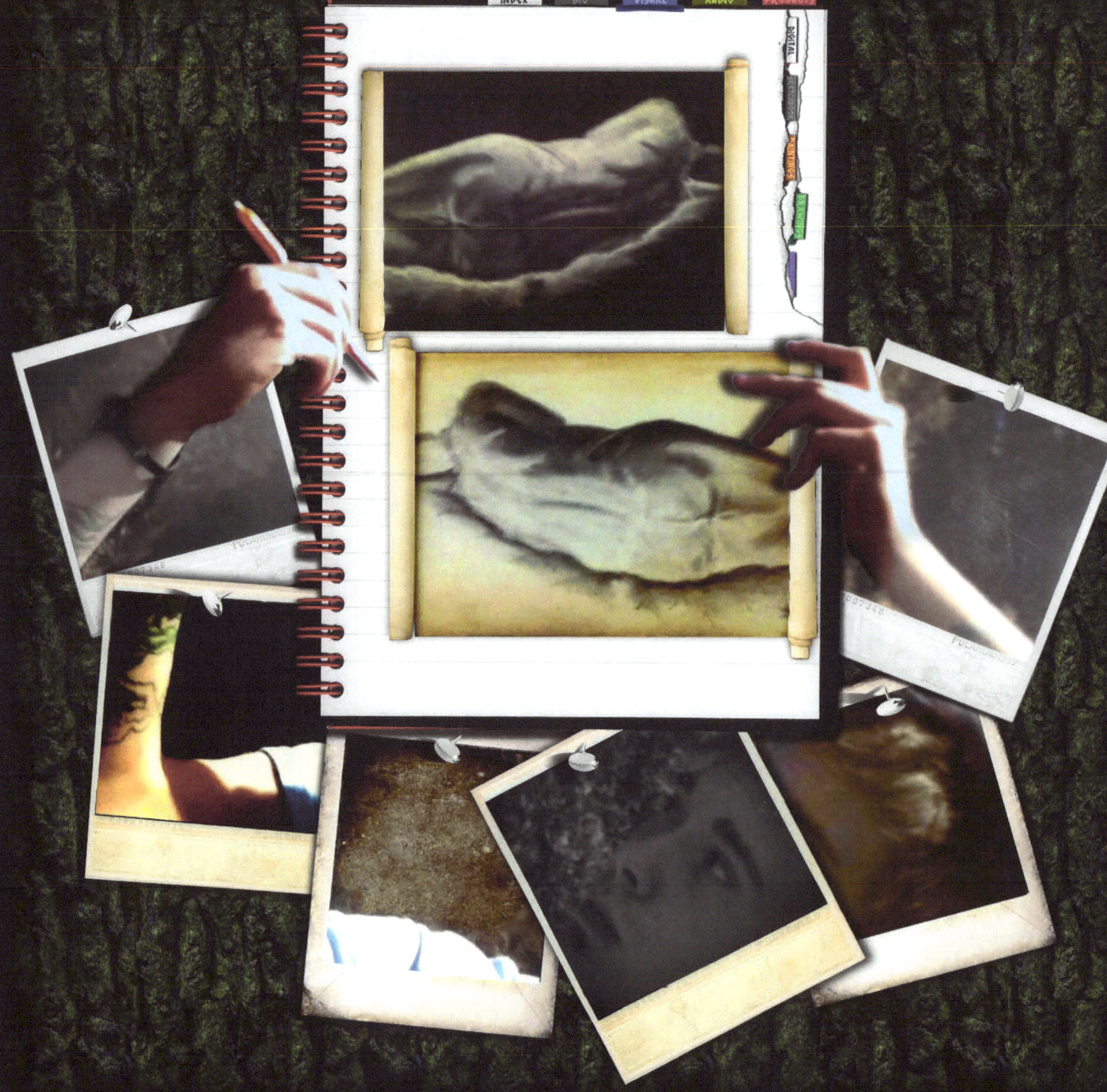
INDEX
BIO
VISUAL
AUDIO
PRODUCTS
DIGITAL
PAINTINGS
DRAWINGS

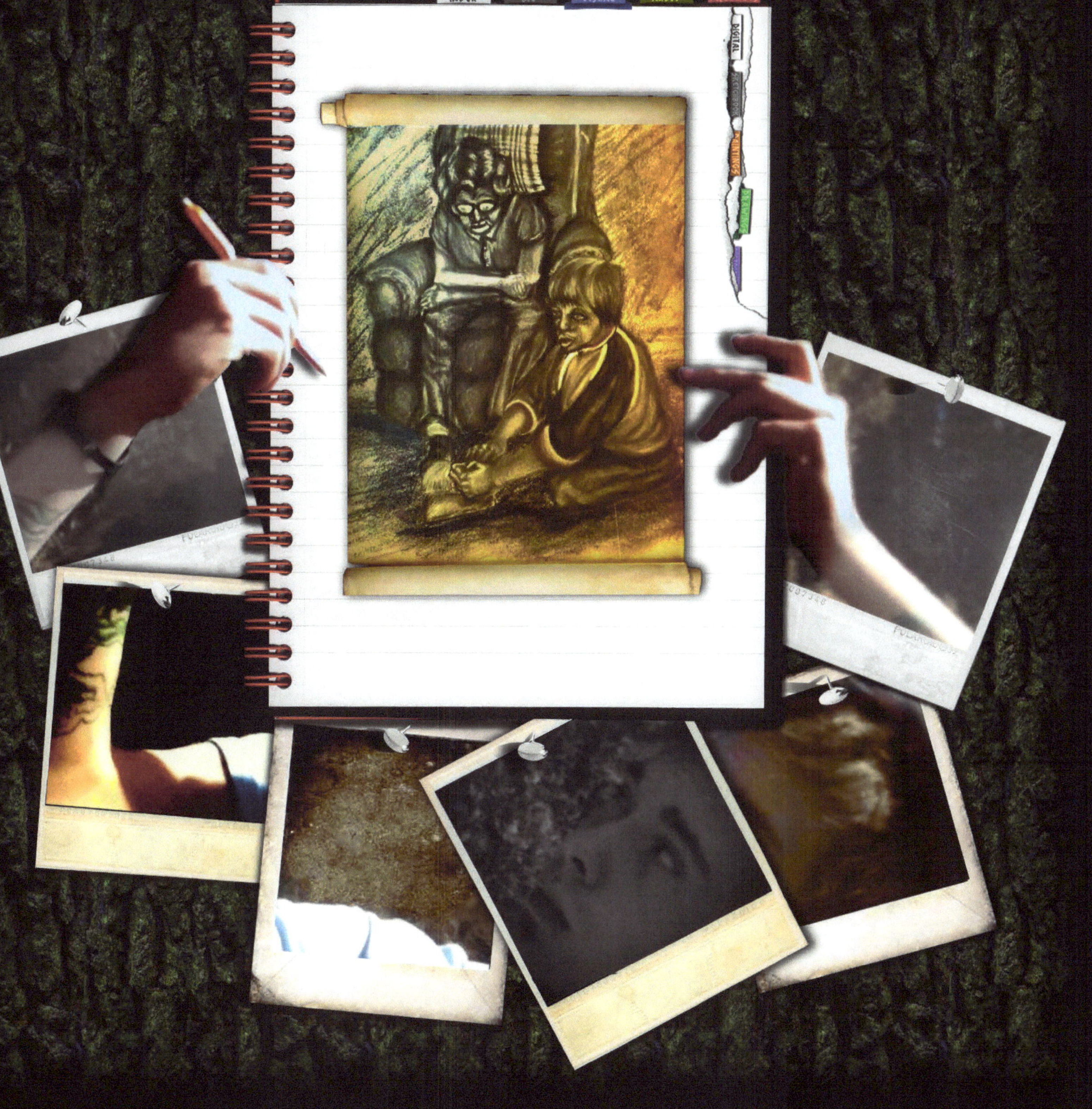
INDEX
BIO
VISUAL
AUDIO
PRODUCTS
DIGITAL
SKETCHBOOK
PAINTINGS
DRAWINGS

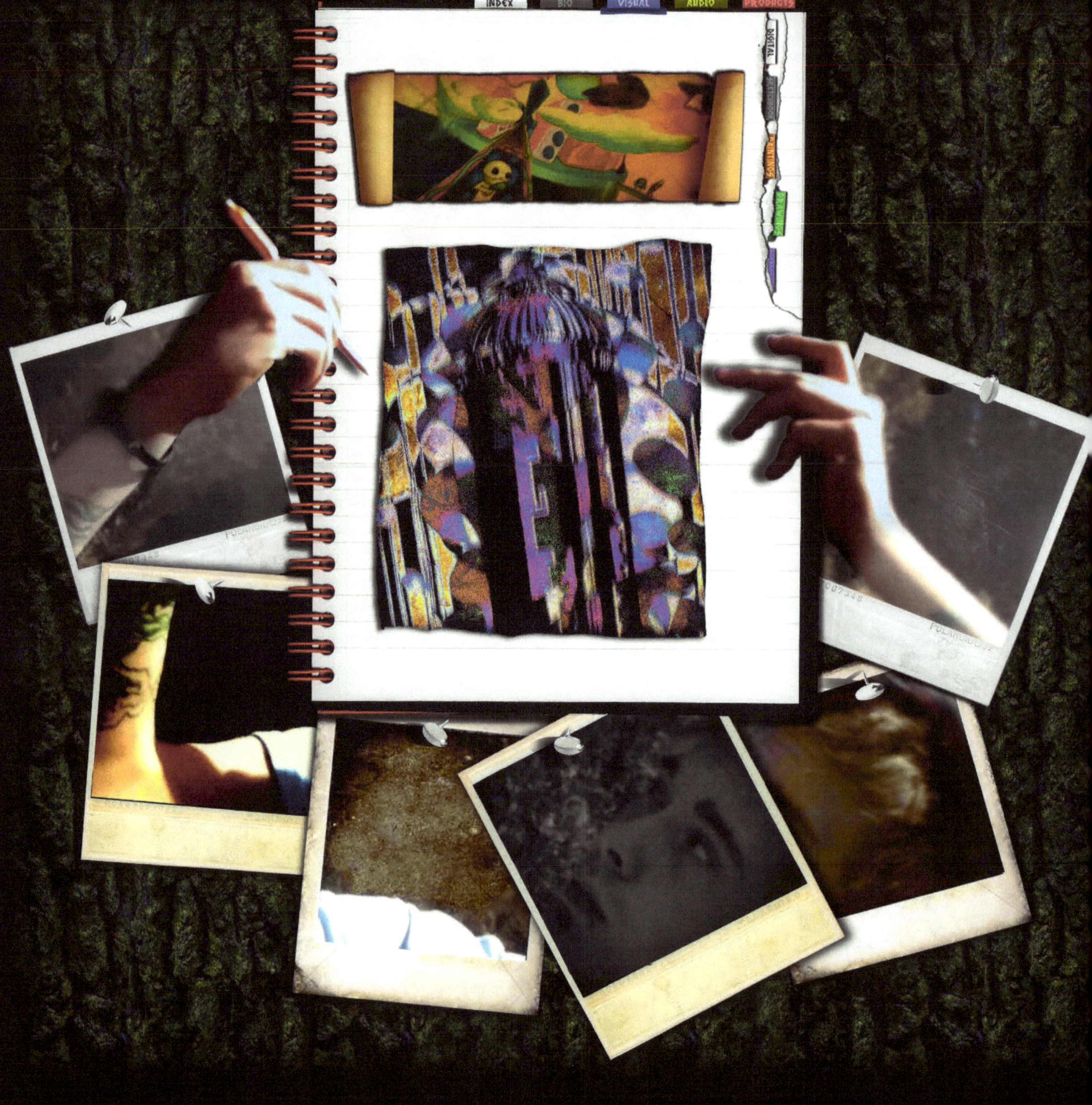
INDEX   BIO   VISUAL   AUDIO   PRODUCTS
DIGITAL
PAINTINGS
DRAWINGS

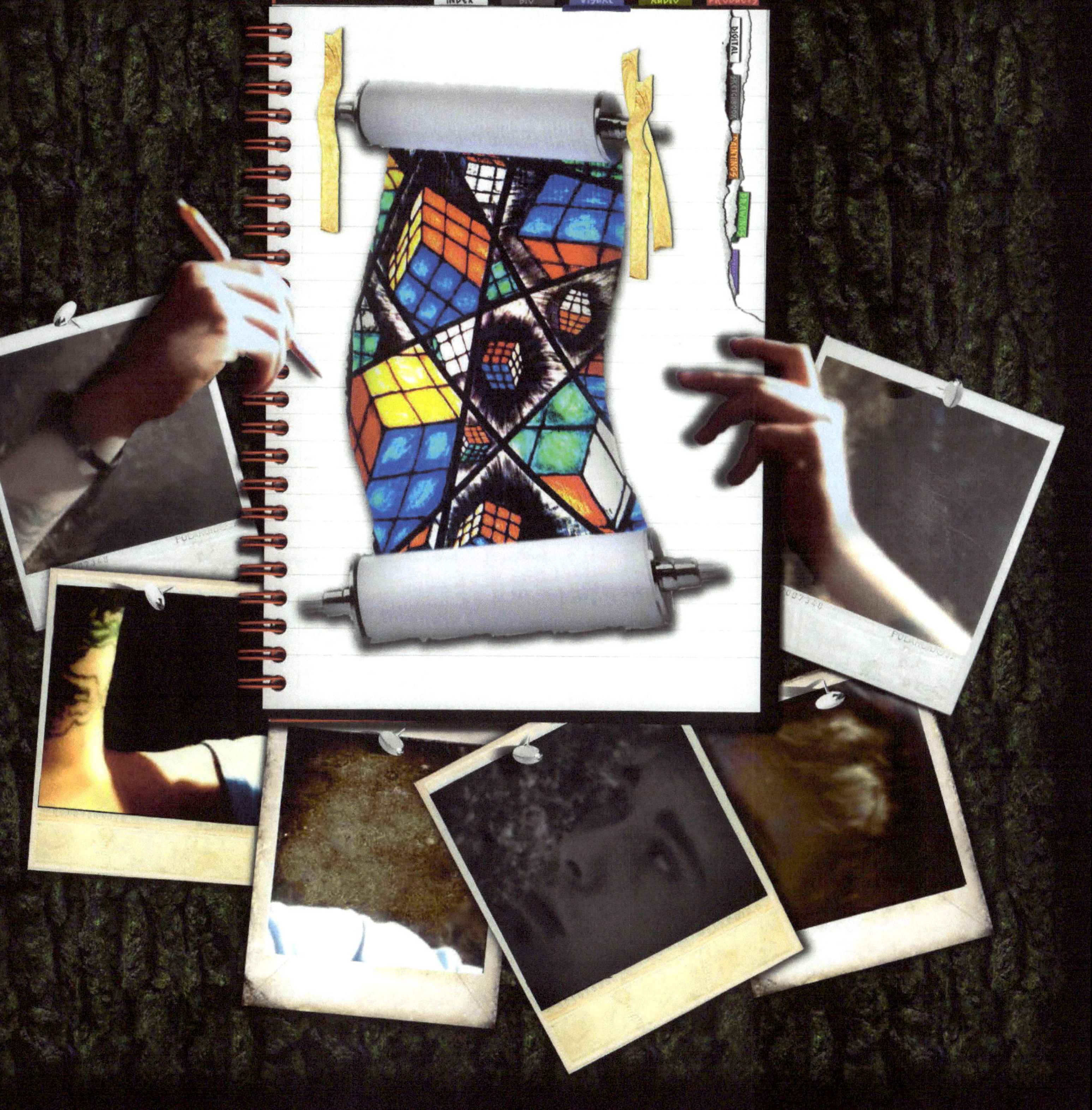

INDEX
BIO
VISUAL
AUDIO
PRODUCTS
DIGITAL
SKETCHBOOK
PAINTINGS
DRAWINGS
POLAROID

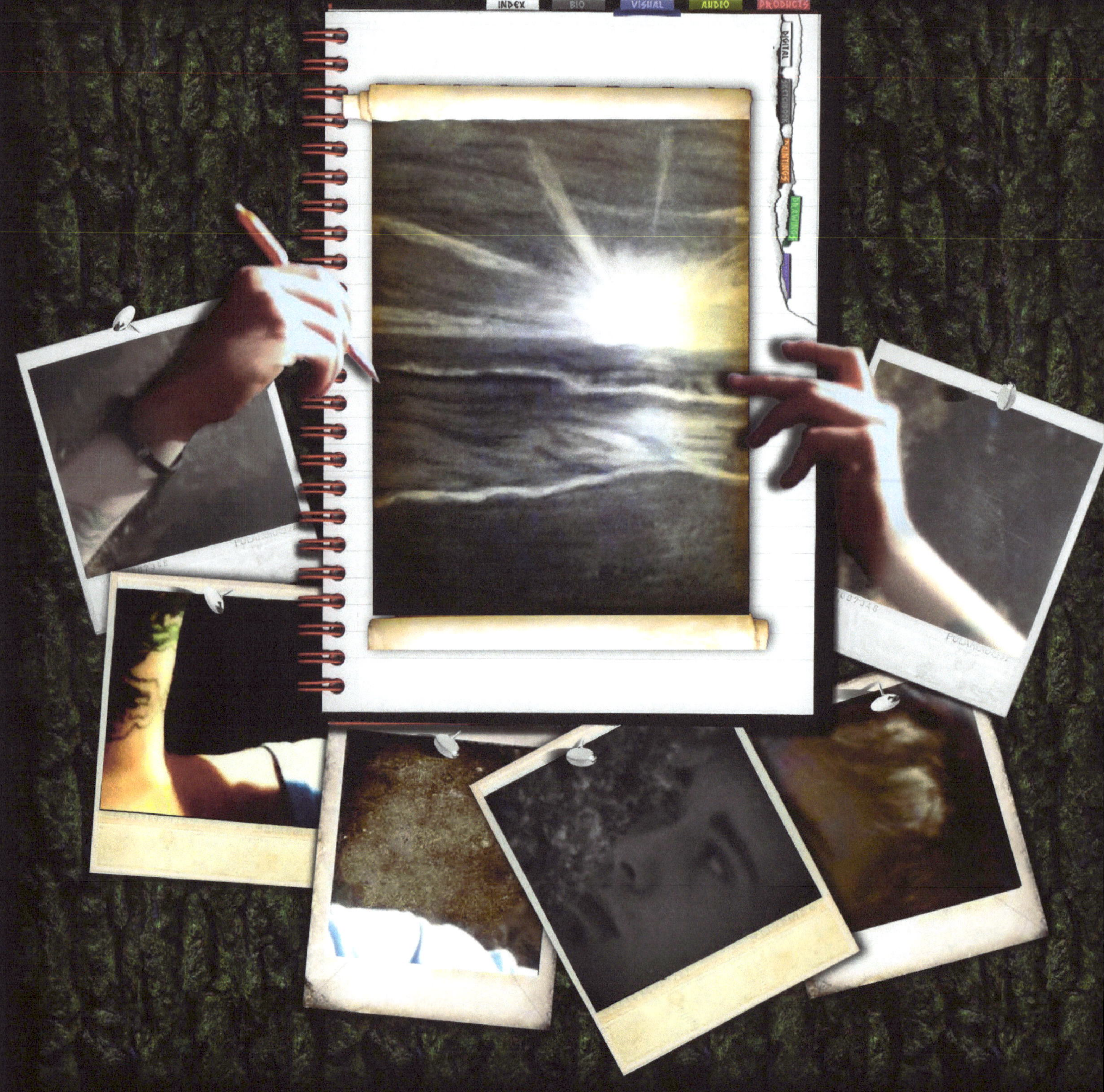

INDEX
BIO
VISUAL
AUDIO
PRODUCTS
DIGITAL
PAINTINGS
DRAWINGS
INDEX
VISUAL
AUDIO
PRODUCTS

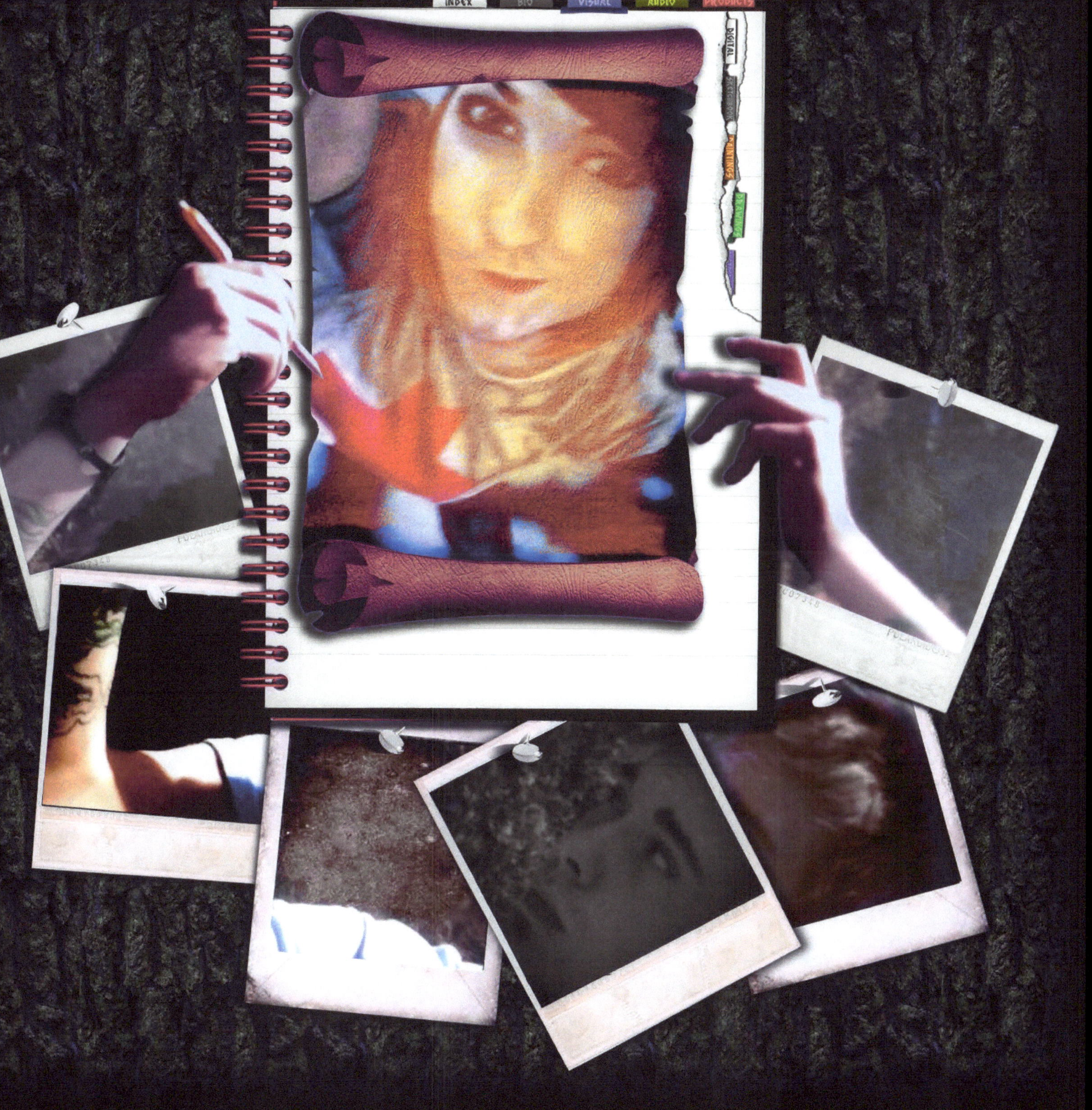

INDEX
BIO
VISUAL
AUDIO
PRODUCTS
DIGITAL
SKETCHBOOK
PAINTINGS
DRAWINGS

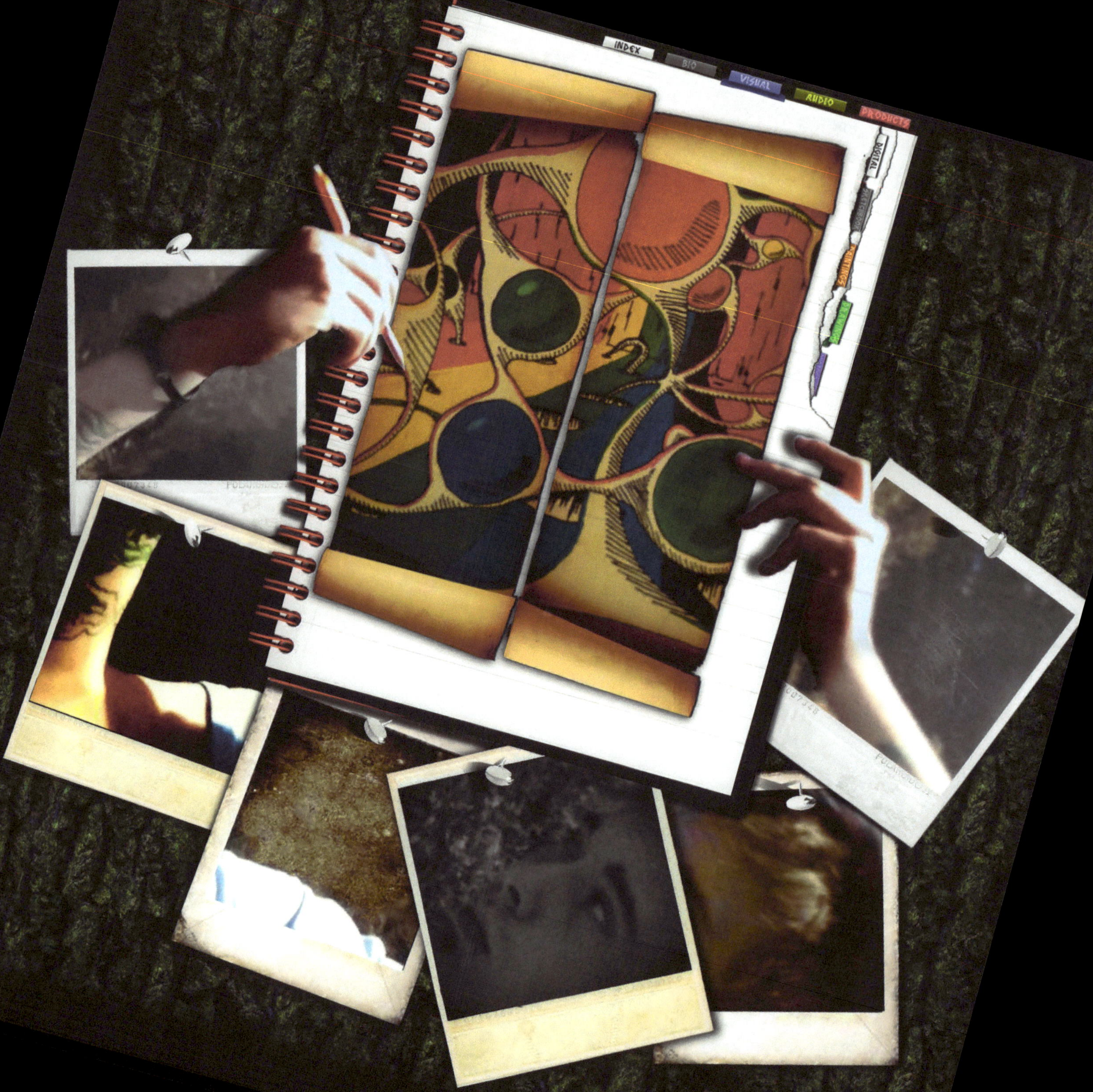
INDEX
BIO
VISUAL
AUDIO
PRODUCTS
DIGITAL

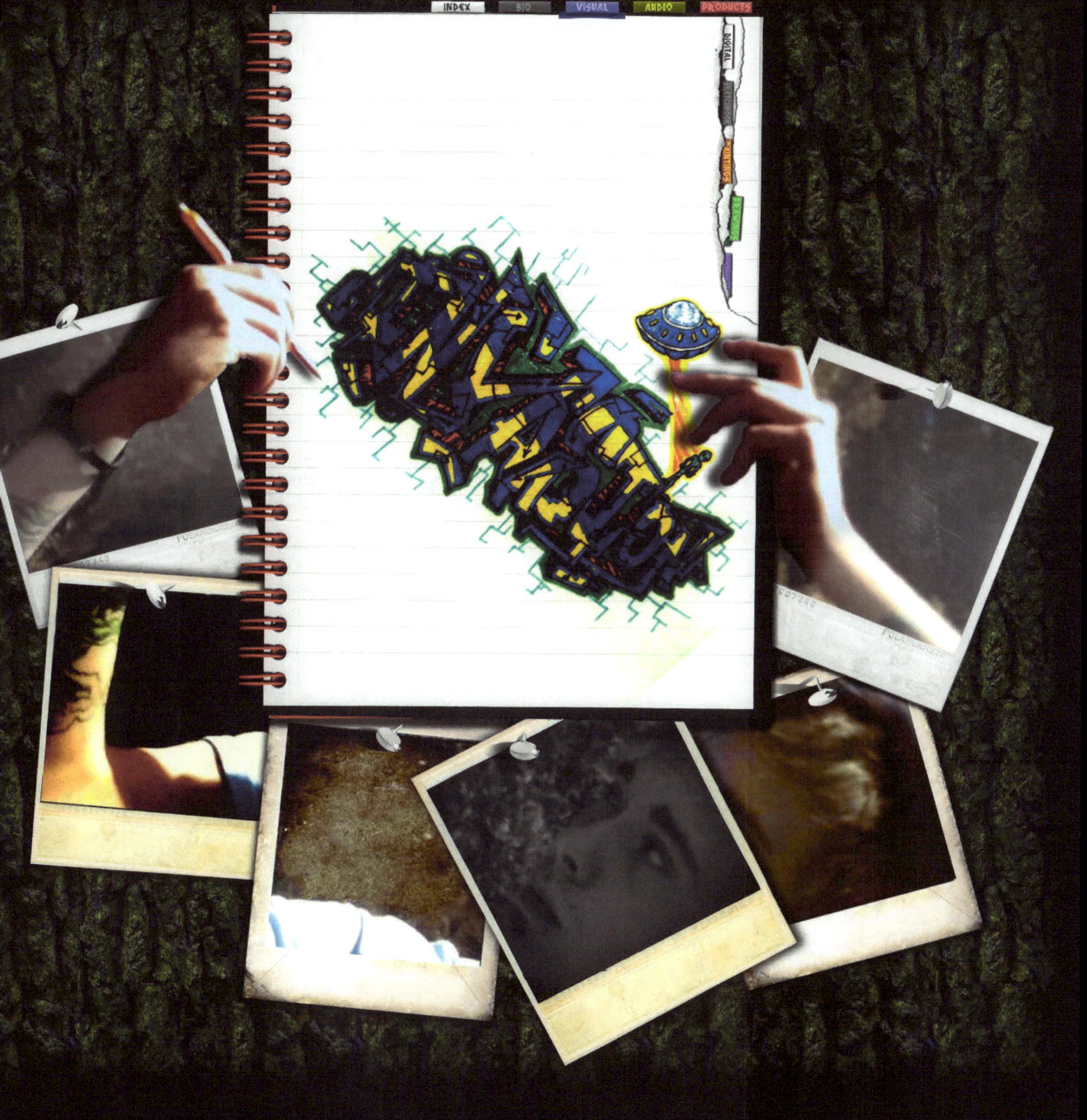

INDEX
BIO
VISUAL
AUDIO
PRODUCTS
DIGITAL
PAINTINGS
DRAWINGS

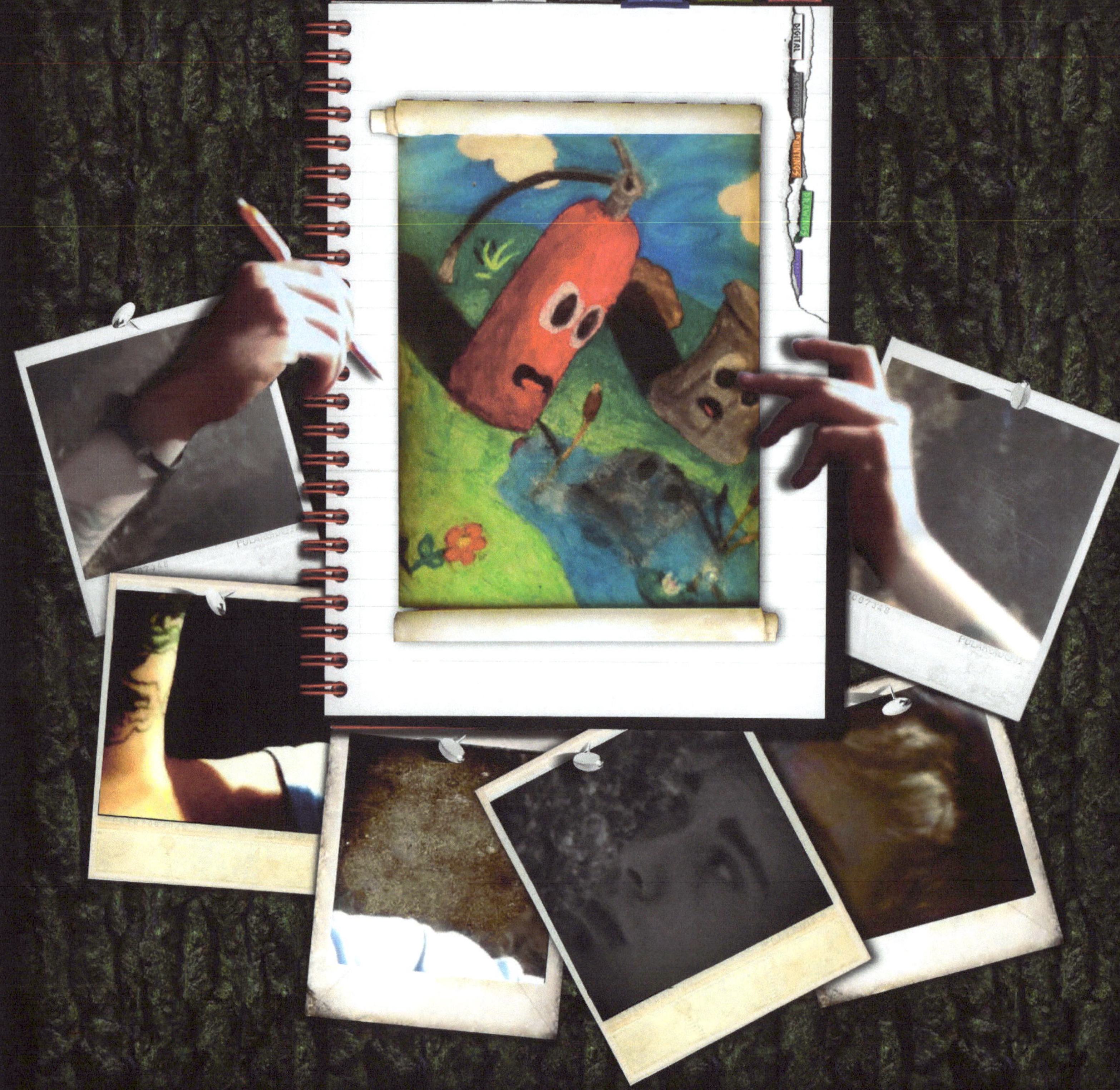

INDEX
BIO
VISUAL
AUDIO
PRODUCTS
DIGITAL
SKETCHBOOK
PAINTINGS
DRAWINGS

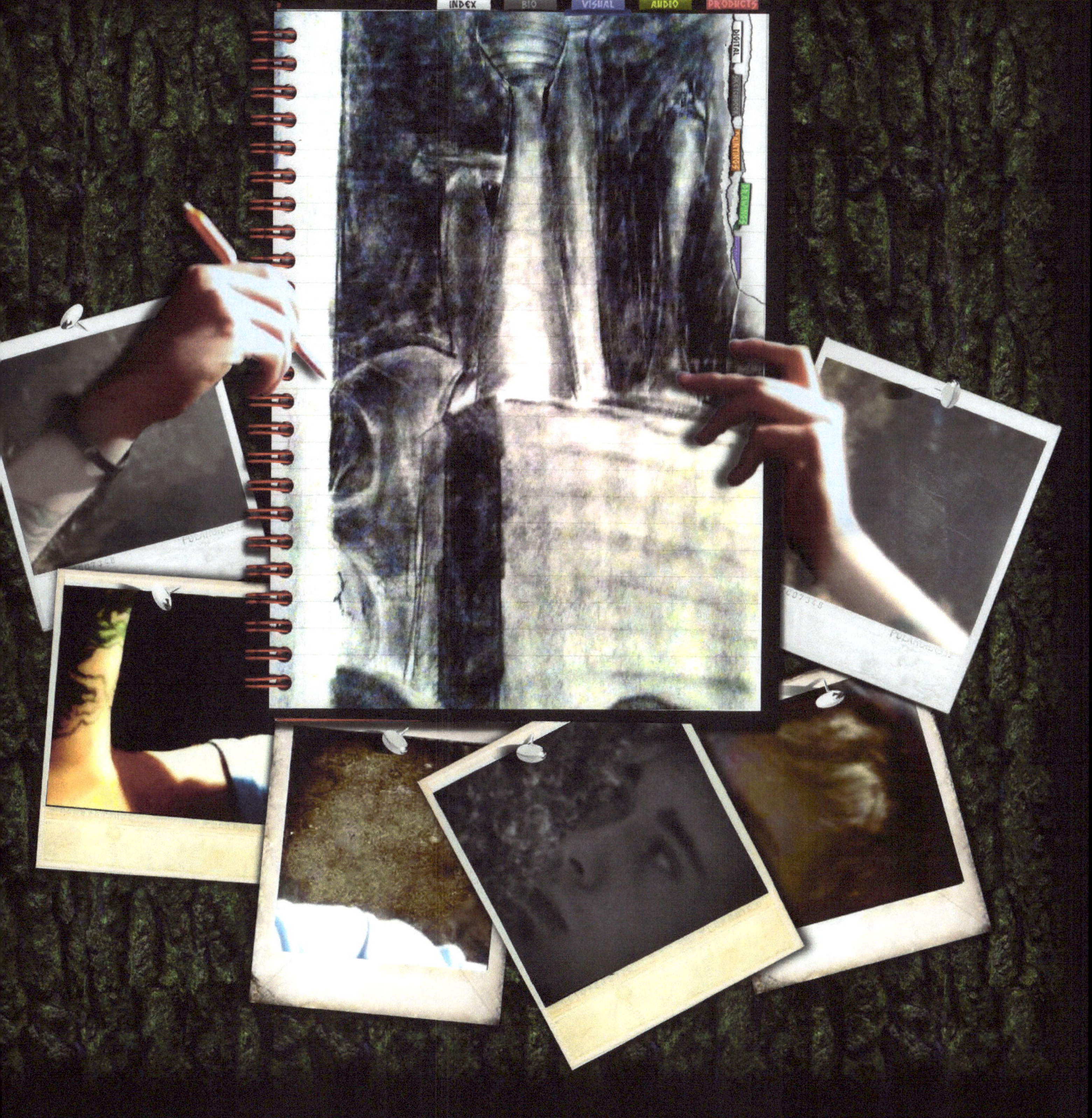

INDEX
BIO
VISUAL
AUDIO
PRODUCTS
DIGITAL
SKETCHBOOK
PAINTINGS
DRAWINGS

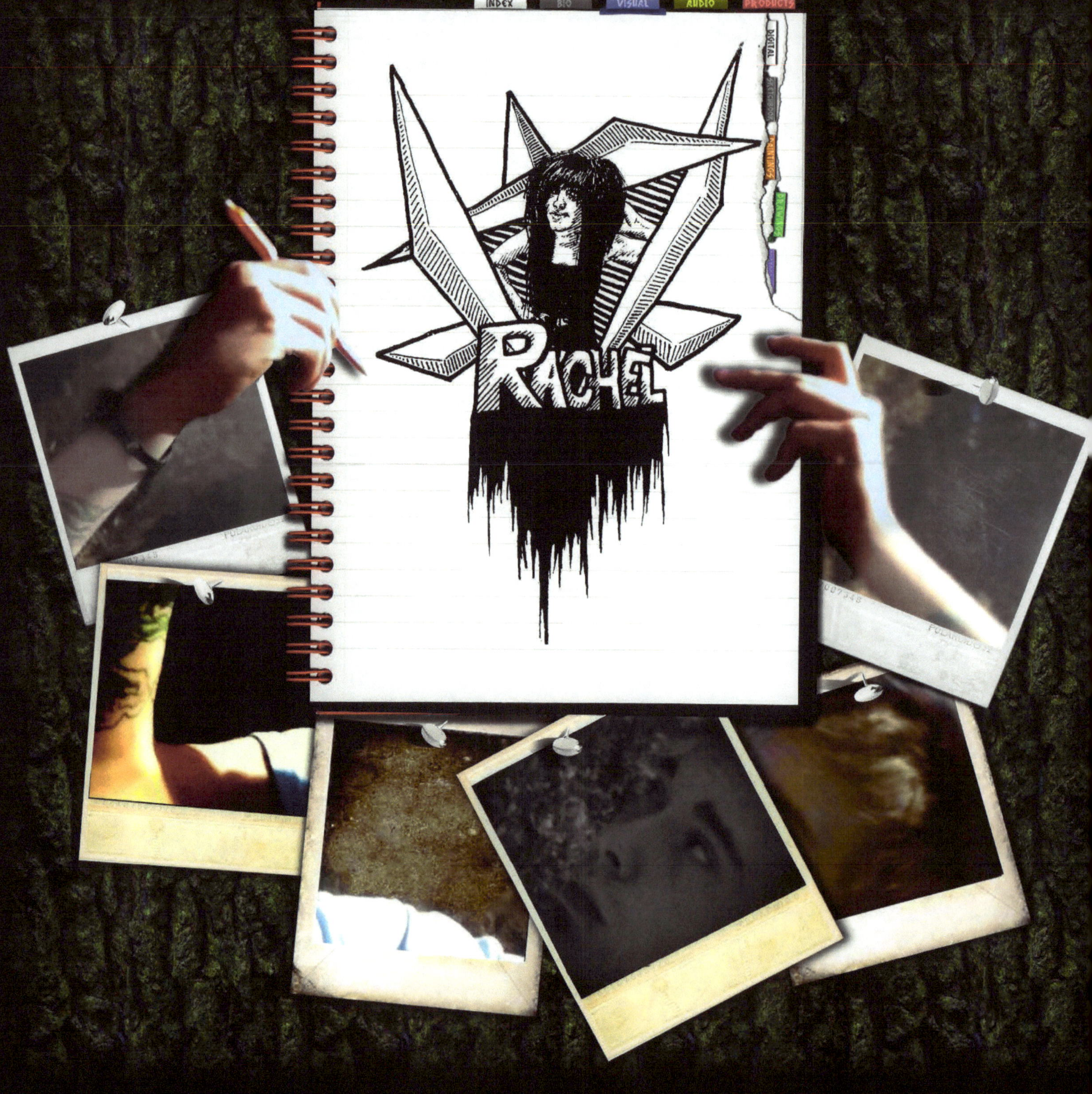
DIGITAL
SKETCHBOOK
PAINTINGS
DRAWINGS
RACHEL

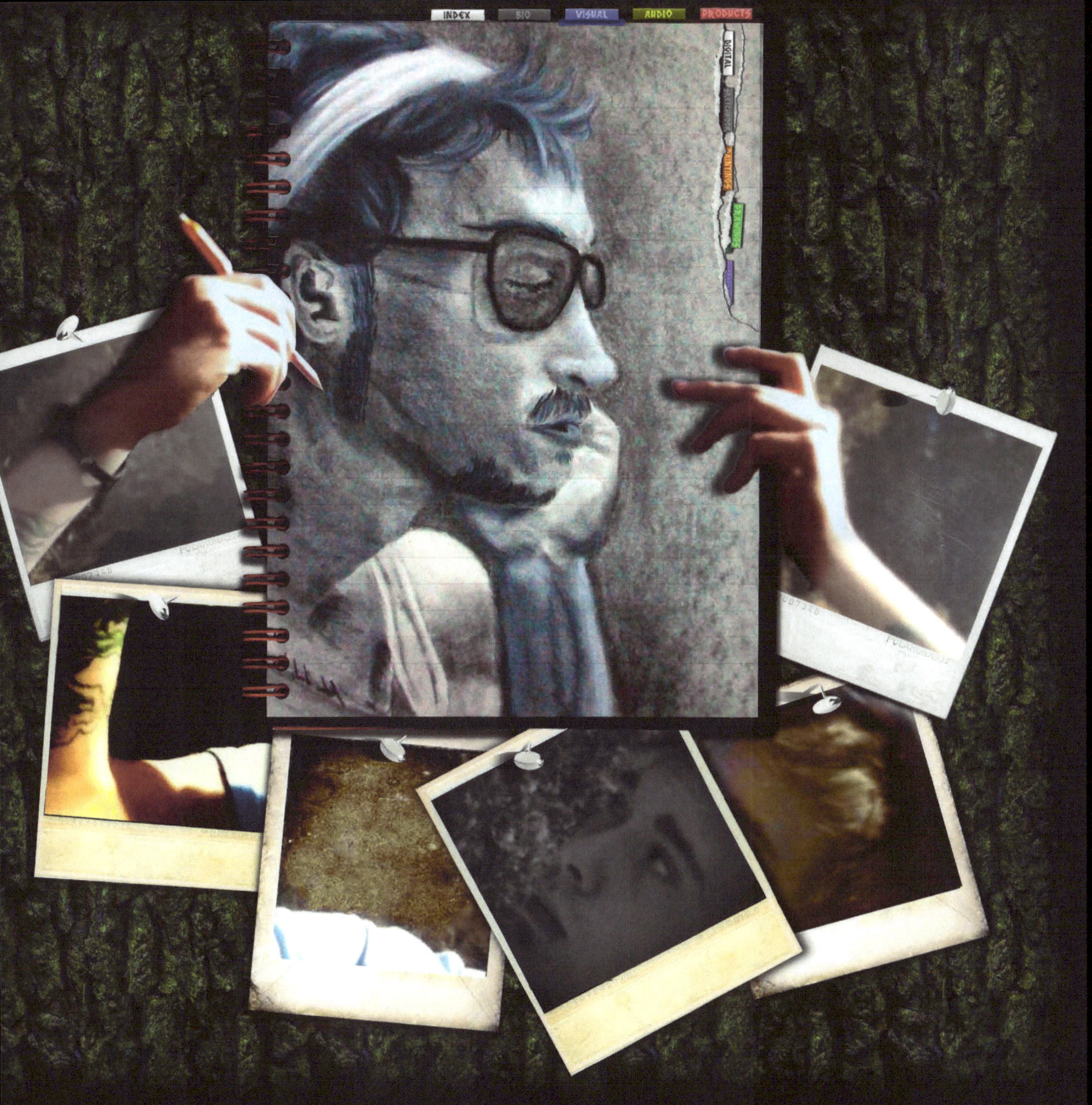

INDEX
BIO
VISUAL
AUDIO
PRODUCTS
DIGITAL
SKETCHBOOK
PAINTINGS
DRAWINGS

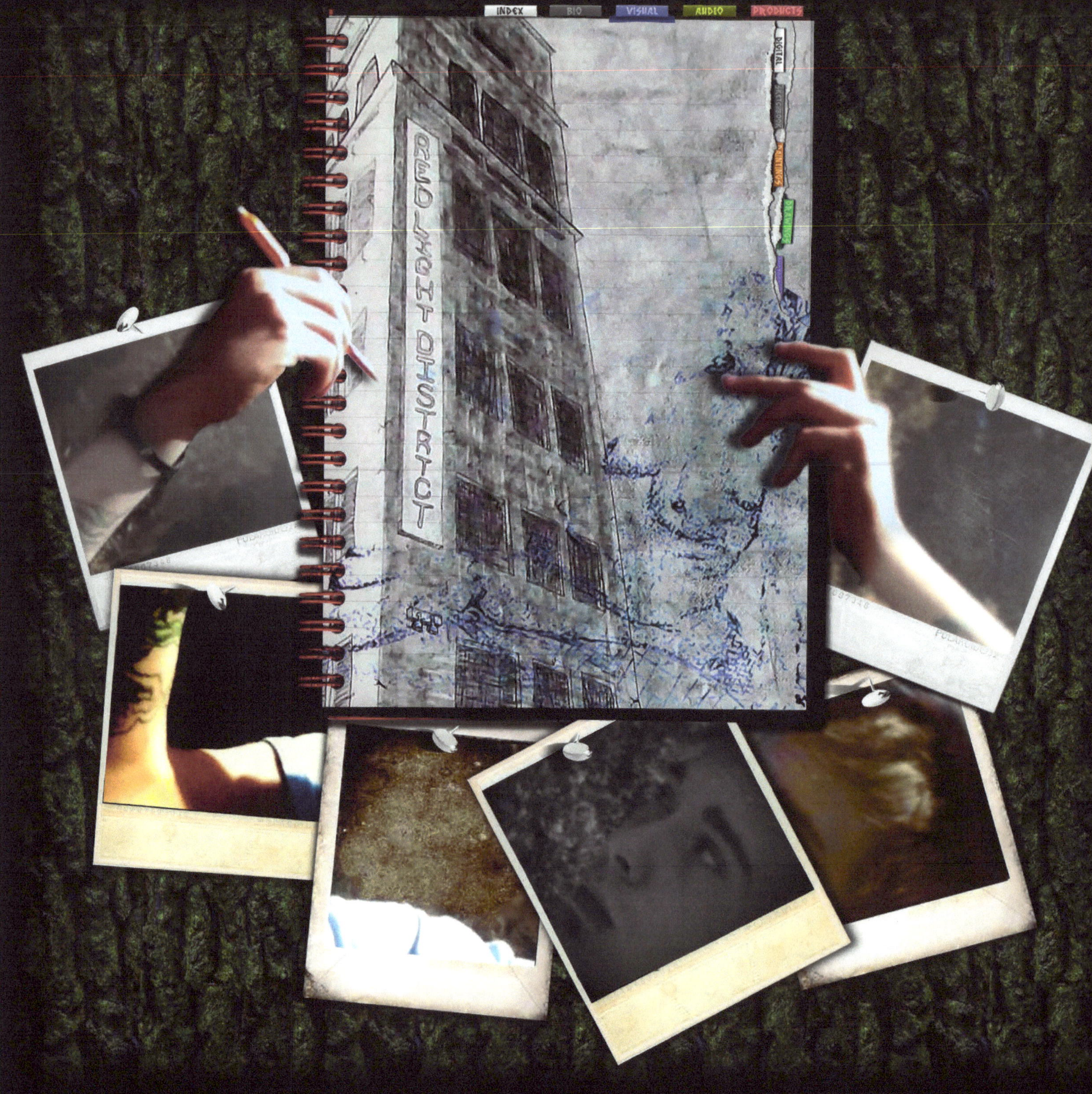
INDEX
BIO
VISUAL
AUDIO
PRODUCTS
DIGITAL
SKETCHES
PAINTINGS
DRAWINGS
RED LIGHT DISTRICT

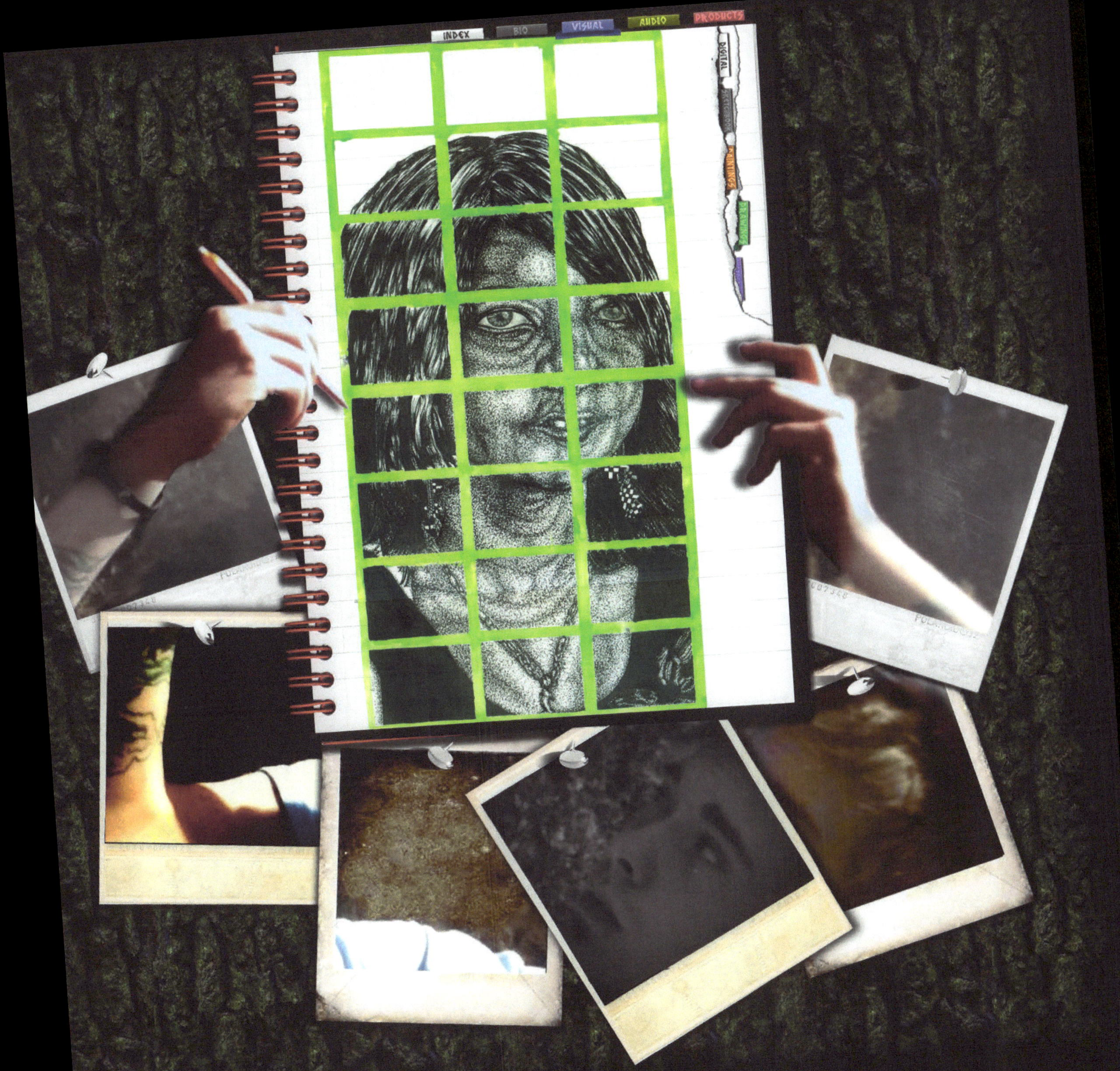
INDEX
BIO
VISUAL
AUDIO
PRODUCTS
DIGITAL
SKETCHBOOK
PAINTINGS

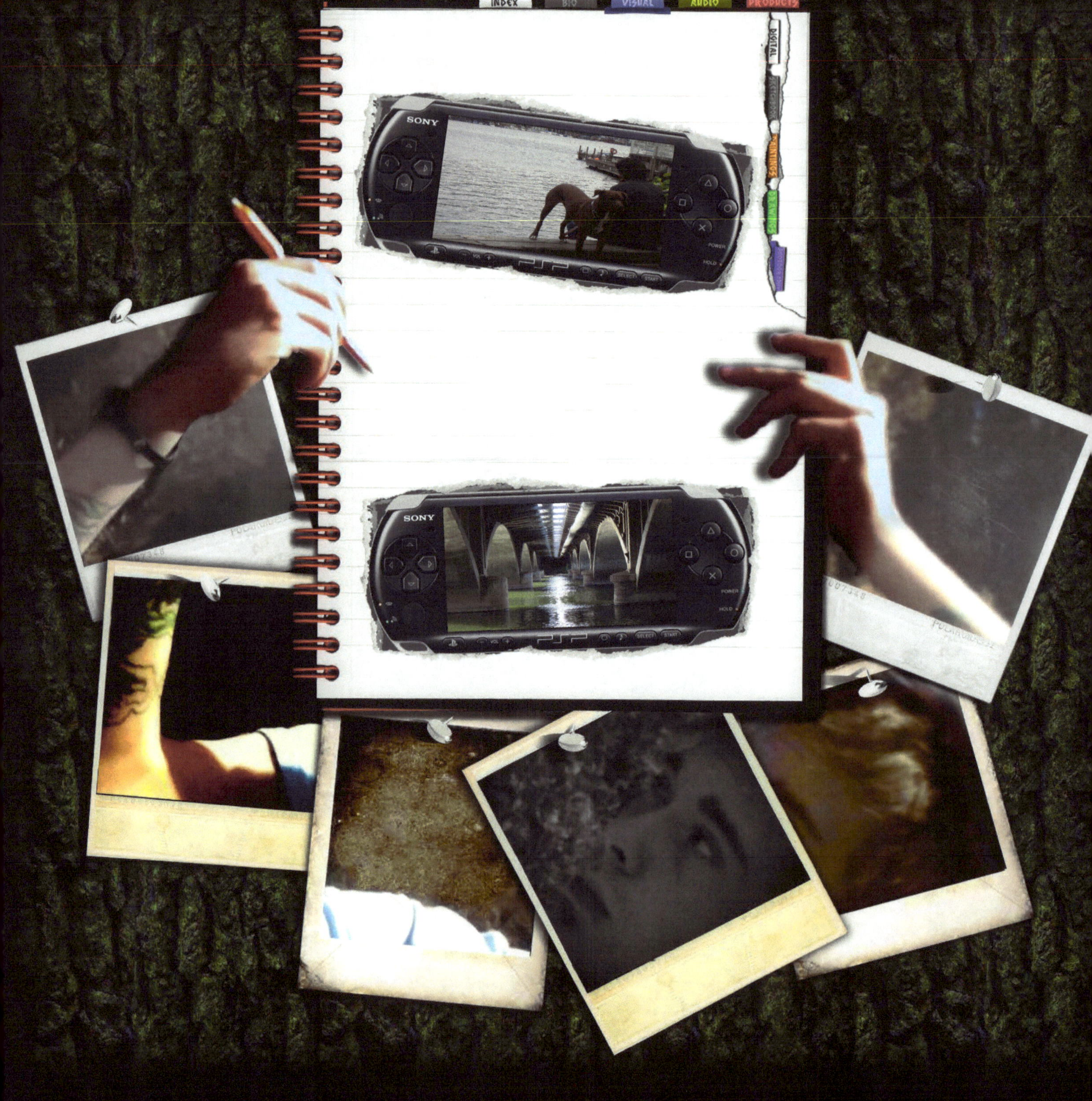
INDEX
BIO
VISUAL
AUDIO
PRODUCTS
DIGITAL
SONY
POWER
HOLD
SELECT
START
SONY
POWER
HOLD
SELECT
START

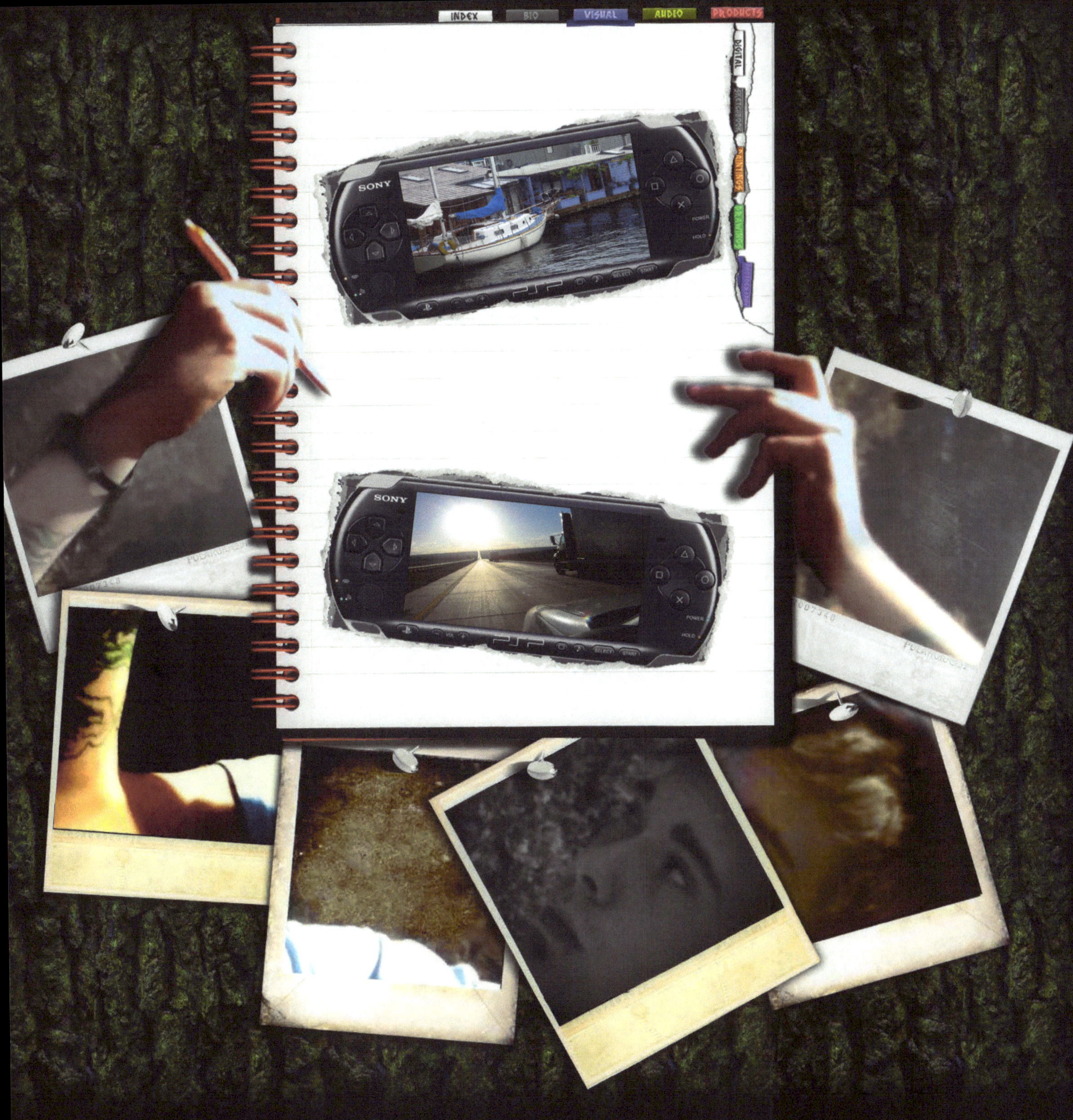

INDEX
BIO
VISUAL
AUDIO
PRODUCTS
DIGITAL
SONY
SONY

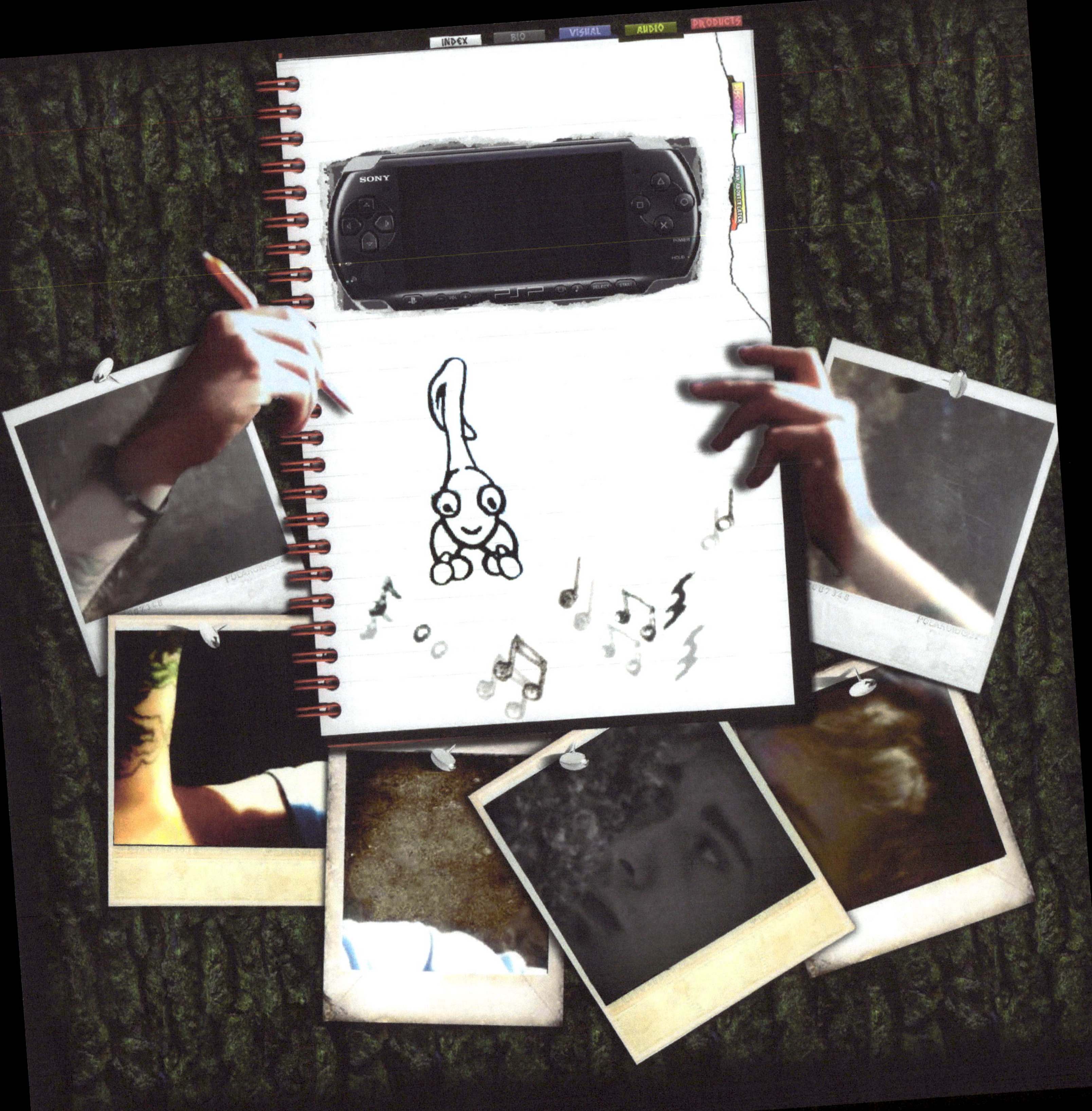
INDEX   BIO   VISUAL   AUDIO   PRODUCTS
SONY

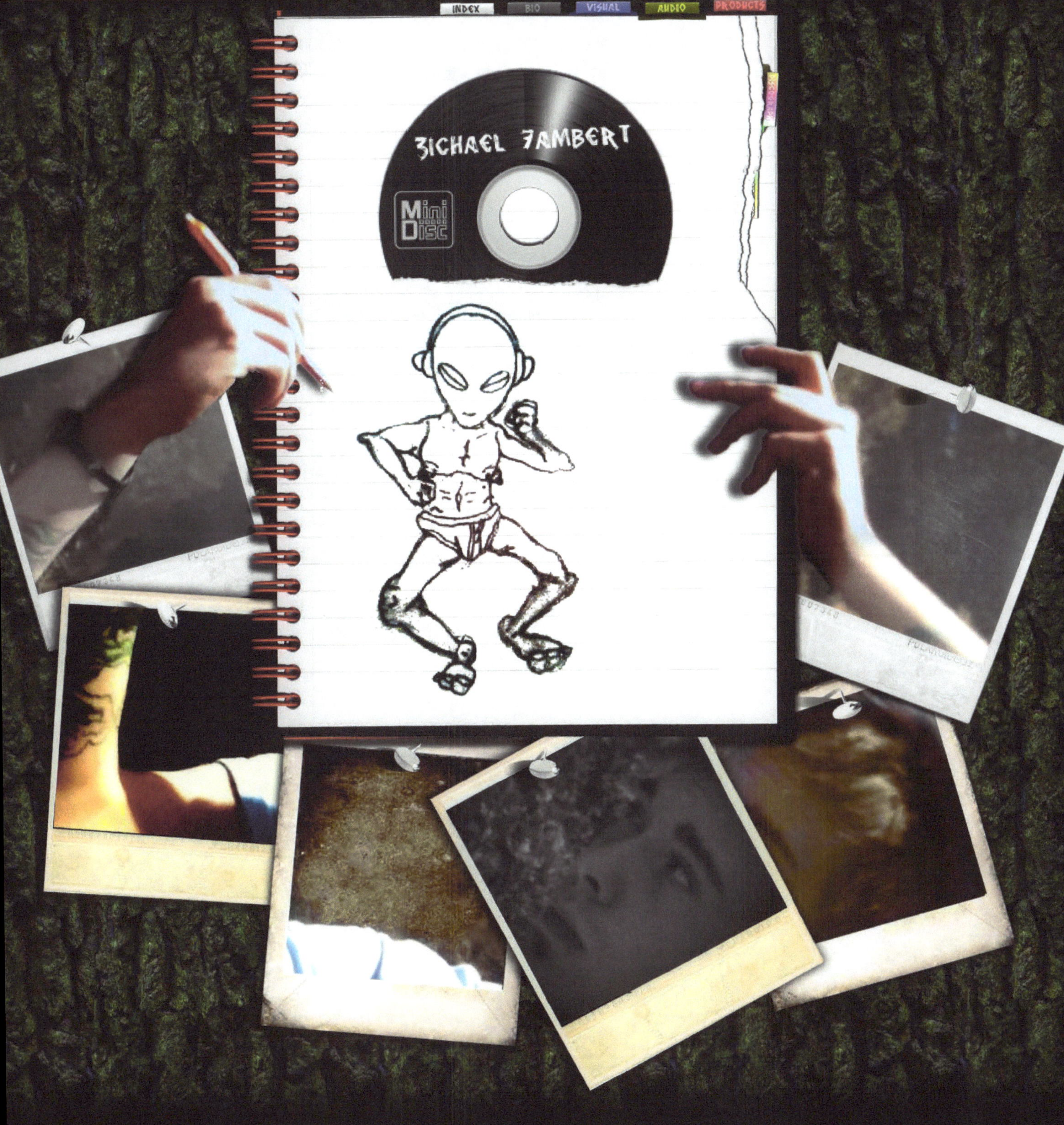
INDEX   BIO   VISUAL   AUDIO   PRODUCTS
ZICHAEL JAMBERT
MiniDisc
INDEX   BIO   VISUAL   AUDIO   PRODUCTS

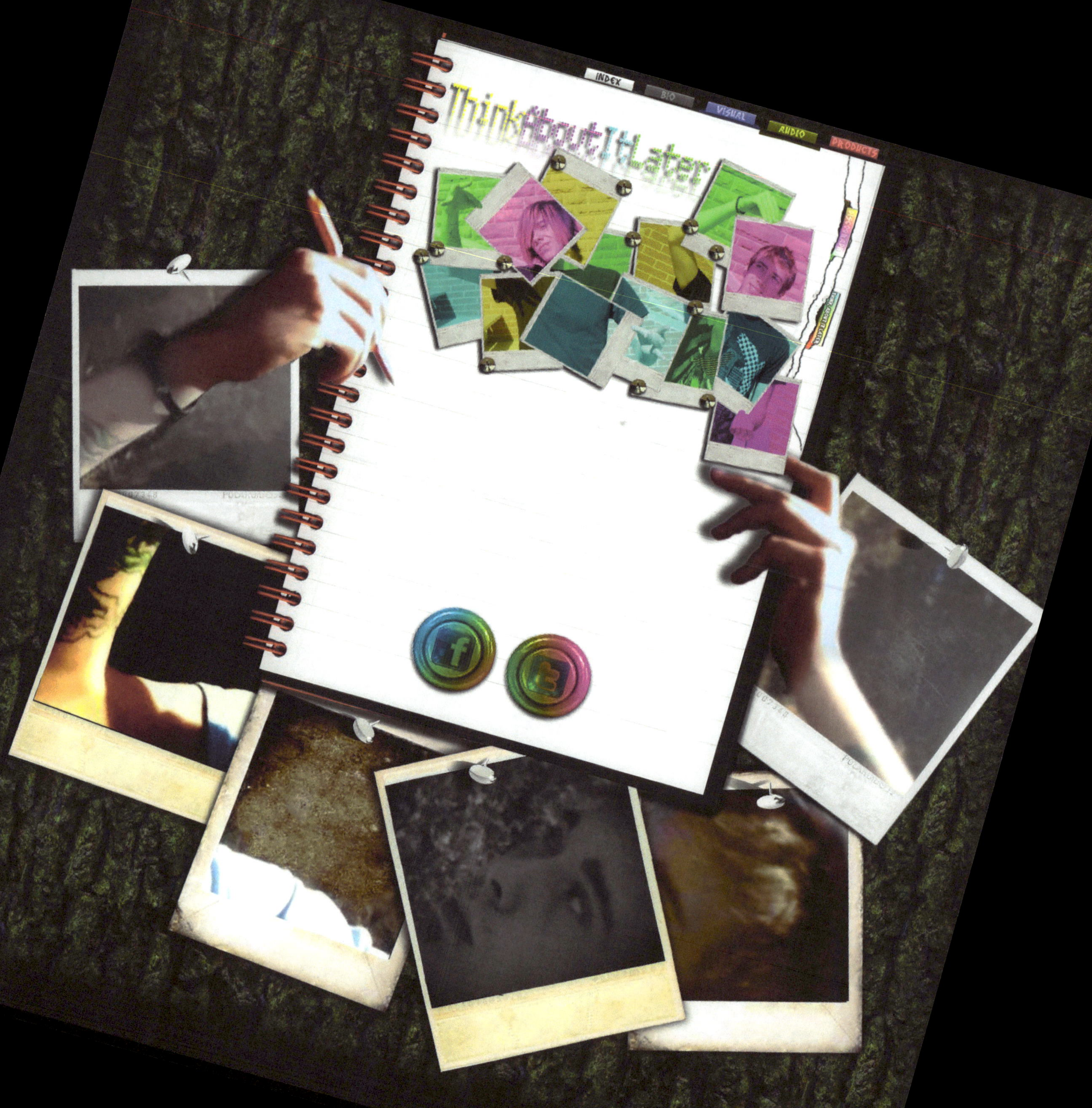

INDEX
BIO
VISUAL
AUDIO
PRODUCTS
ThinkAboutItLater

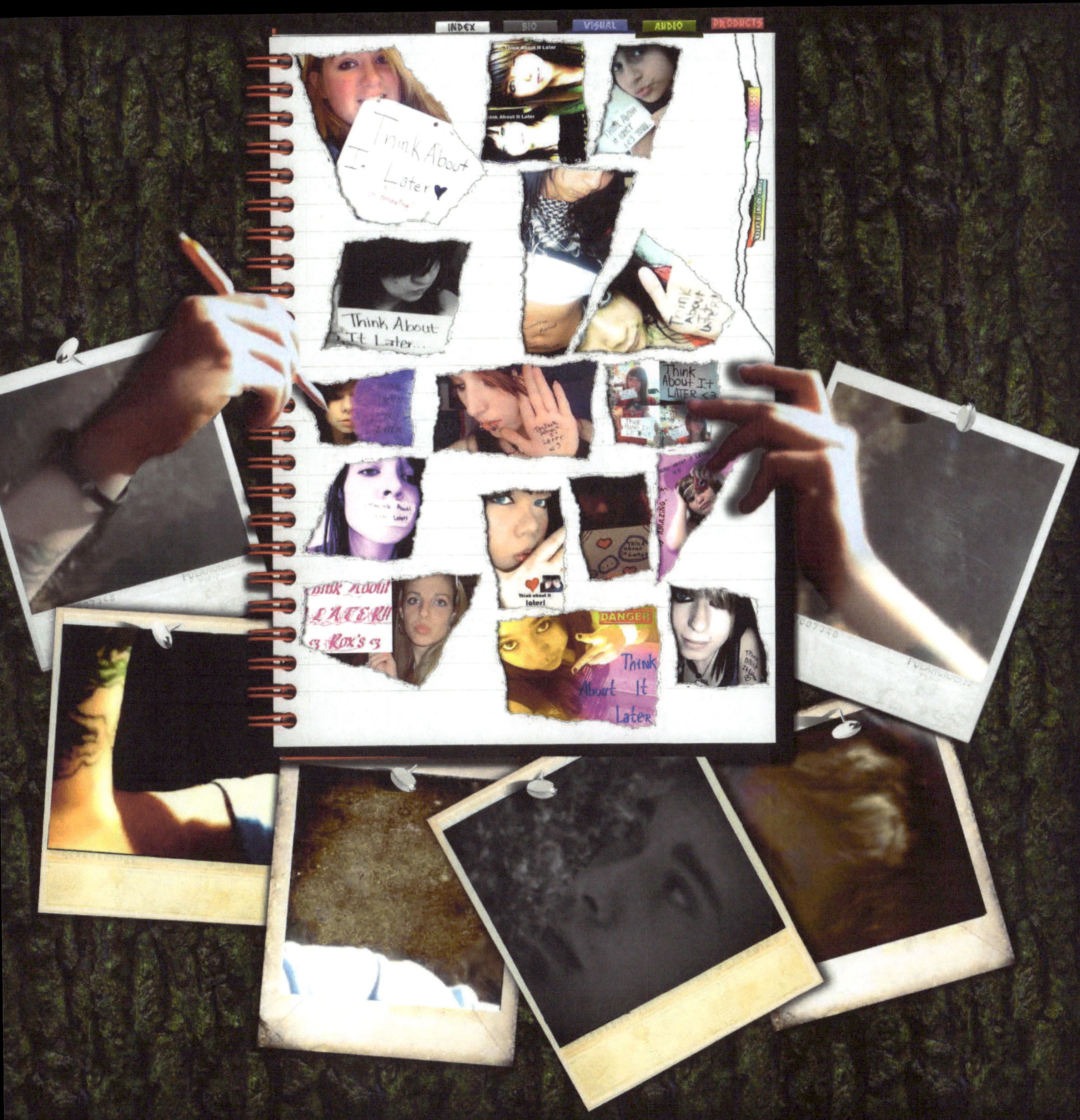

INDEX
BIO
VISUAL
AUDIO
PRODUCTS
Think About It Later
Think About I. Later
Think About It Later...
Think About It LATER <3
Think About It Later <3
Think About It Later!
Think About It LATER!! 3 Rox's 3
DANGER
Think About It Later
Think about it later!

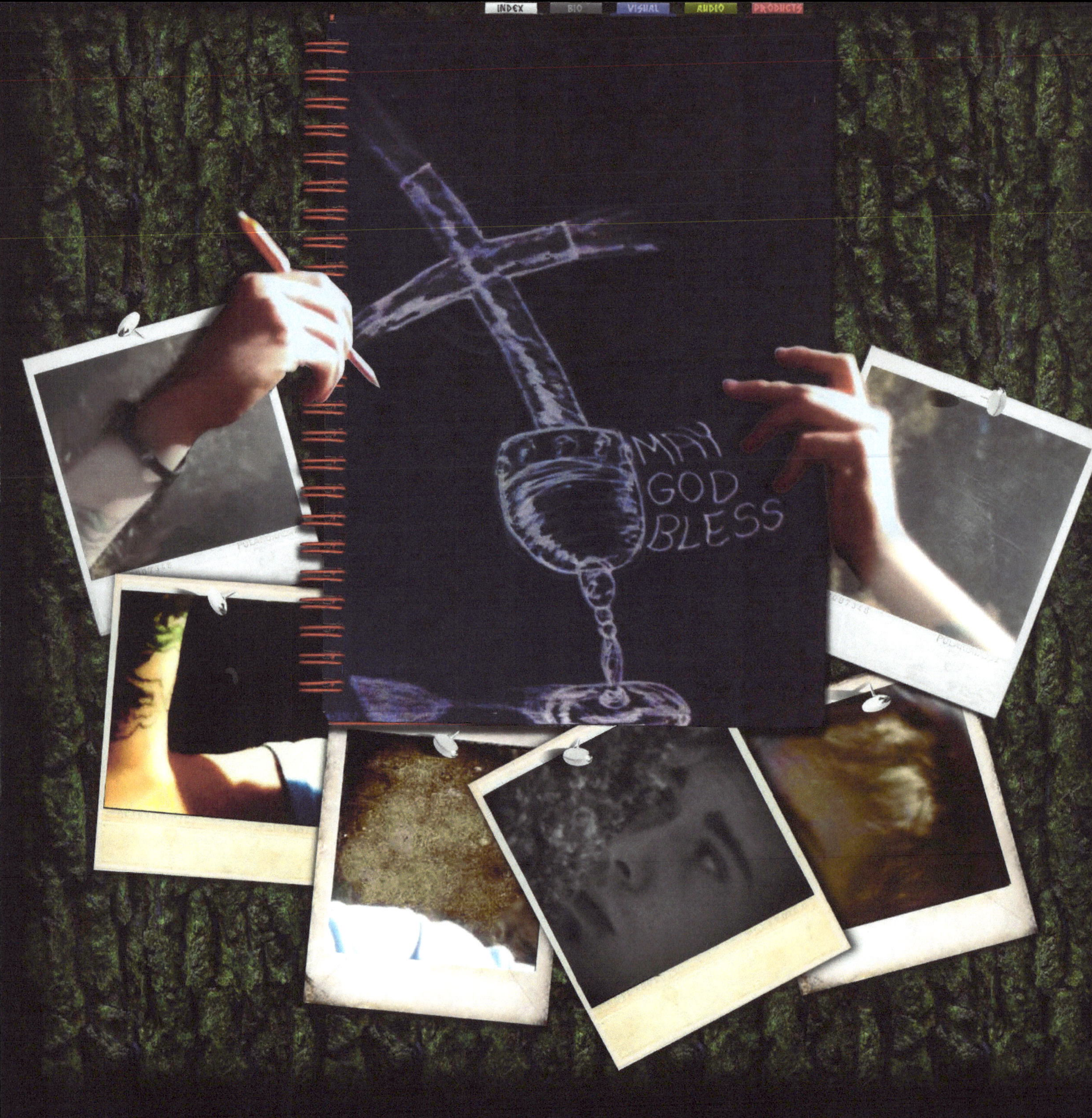
INDEX BIO VISUAL AUDIO PRODUCTS
MAY
GOD
BLESS

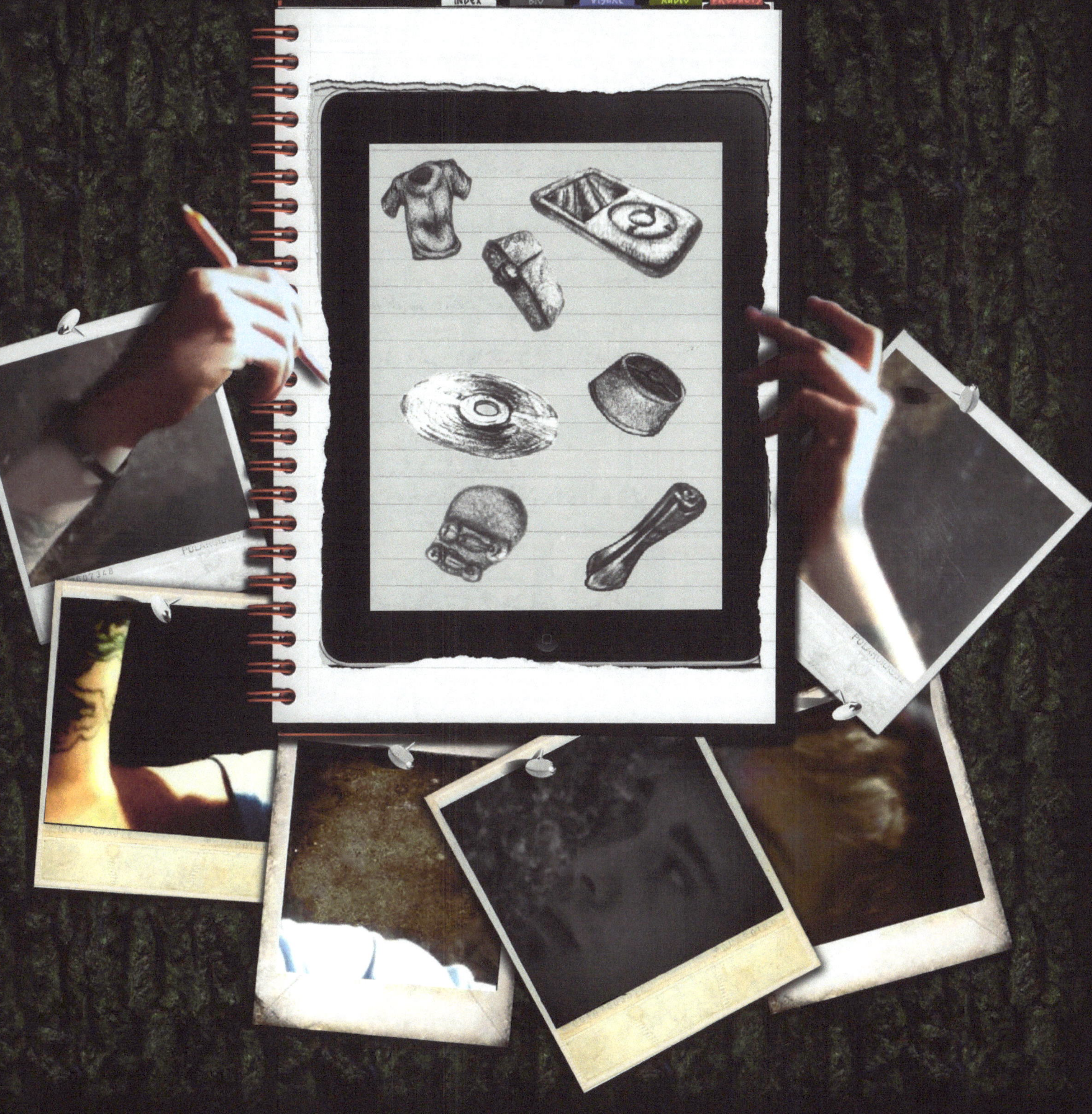

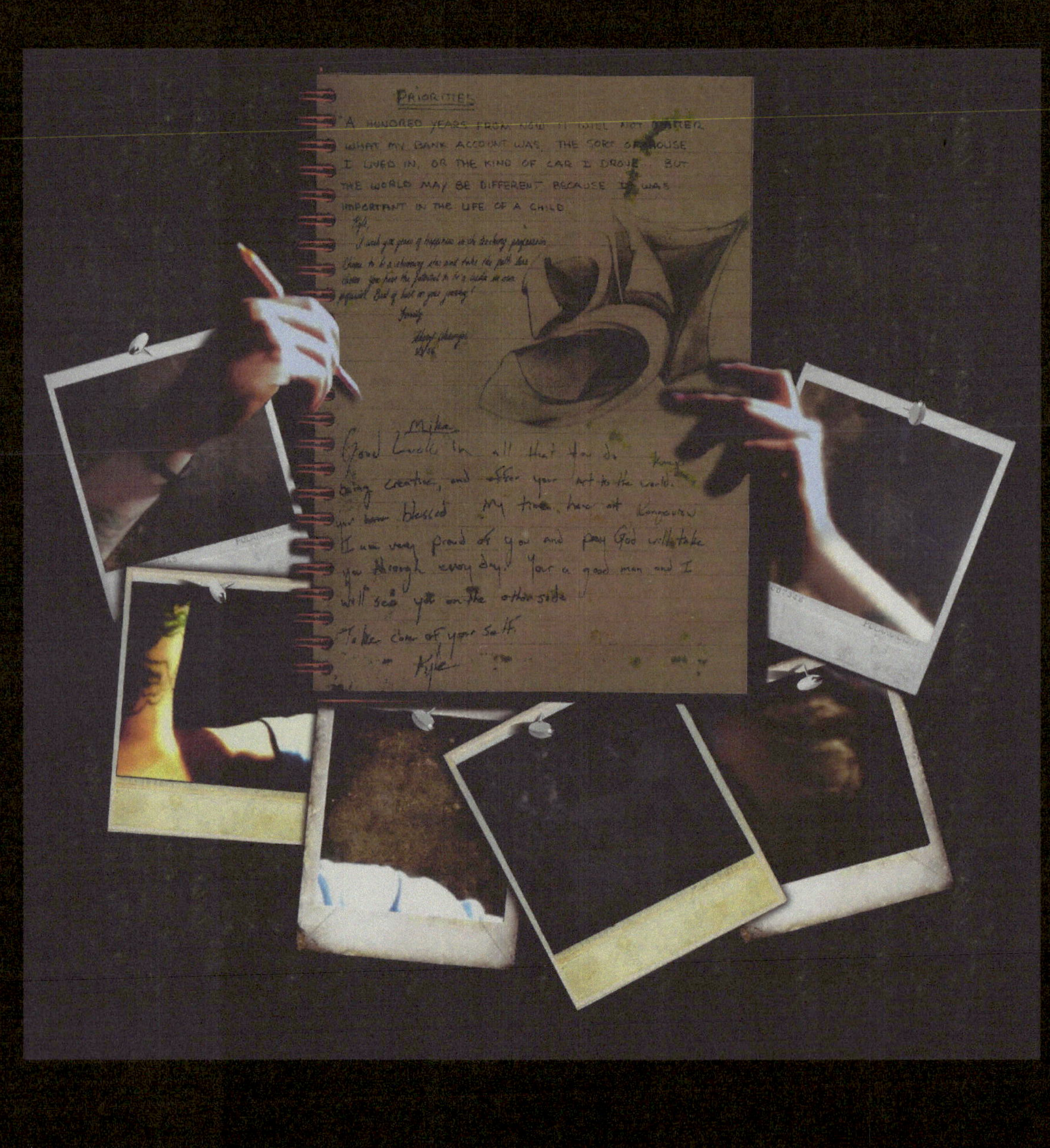
PRIORITIES
A HUNDRED YEARS FROM NOW IT WILL NOT MATTER
WHAT MY BANK ACCOUNT WAS, THE SORT OF HOUSE
I LIVED IN, OR THE KIND OF CAR I DROVE. BUT
THE WORLD MAY BE DIFFERENT BECAUSE I WAS
IMPORTANT IN THE LIFE OF A CHILD
Mike,
Good Luck in all that you do
being creative, and offer your art to the world.
your been blessed. My time here at Longview
I am very proud of you and pray God will take
you through every day. Your a good man and I
will see you on the other side
Take care of your self.
— Kyle

www.ingramcontent.com/pod-product-compliance
Lightning Source LLC
Chambersburg PA
CBHW041644110726
48005CB00003B/695